GREEN GRAPHIC DESIGN

GREEN GRAPHIC DESIGN

BRIAN DOUGHERTY WITH CELERY DESIGN COLLABORATIVE

ALLWORTH PRESS
NEW YORK

To Aiko and the Class of 2021

This book is printed with low-VOC vegetable-based inks by Thomson-Shore, an FSC-certified printer and a member of the Green Press Initiative. It is printed on 100 percent post-consumer recycled paper made with renewable energy by Mohawk Paper Company.

© 2008 Brian Dougherty

12 11 10 09 08 5 4 3 2 1

Published by Allworth Press
An imprint of Allworth Communications, Inc.
10 East 23rd Street, New York, NY 10010

Cover design by Celery Design Collaborative
Interior design by Celery Design Collaborative
Page composition/typography by Celery Design Collaborative

ISBN-13: 978-1-58115-511-2
ISBN-10: 1-58115-511-5

Library of Congress Cataloging-in-Publication Data:
    Dougherty, Brian.
    Green graphic design / by Brian Dougherty ; with Celery Design Collaborative.
    p. cm.
    Includes bibliographical references and index.
    ISBN-13: 978-1-58115-511-2 (alk. paper)
    ISBN-10: 1-58115-511-5 (alk. paper)
1. Commercial art—Environmental aspects. I. Celery Design Collaborative. II. Title.
NC997.D64 2008
741.6—dc22   200803442

Printed in the United States of America

CONTENTS

ACKNOWLEDGMENTS

Many thanks to my wife Patricia Katsura, for her love, patience, and energetic sketches. Thanks to my friend and business partner Rod DeWeese, for constant support and counsel. Thanks also to Sophia Traweek and Bob Porter, both of whom provided valuable feedback on the content and structure of this story, and to Gil Friend, Phil Hamlett, and Jeff Towner, who reviewed various parts of the text. The whole team at Celery helped enormously with research and design, especially Yoonju Chung, who contributed countless hours to this project. Thanks also to the many people who provided information, advice, and inspiring examples of green design from around the world.

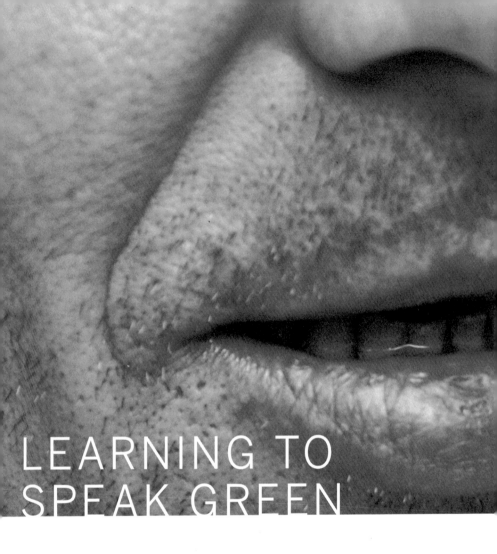

LEARNING TO
SPEAK GREEN

I had my first introduction to green design from an architect. In 1995, a California architect named Sim Van der Ryn published a book called *Ecological Design* that sparked my interest. It talked about using the power of design to create innovative solutions for a set of pressing ecological problems. For a while, I thought I might shift my career from graphic design to architecture, which seemed to be where eco-innovative design was happening.

Then I came across a book called *From Eco-cities to Living Machines* by John and Nancy Todd, which talked about

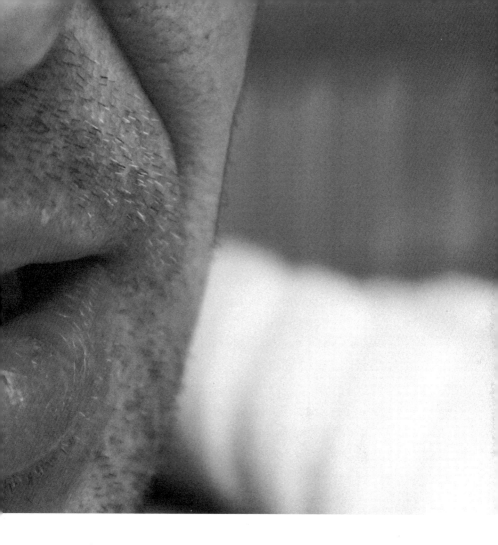

ecological design from an engineer's perspective. At the time, I worked down the street from the restaurant Chez Panisse, where Alice Waters crafted some of America's most celebrated cuisine by combining culinary innovation and ecological responsibility through the use of local, seasonal ingredients. This struck me as the gastronomic equivalent of ecological design. Paul Hawken's book, *Ecology of Commerce,* expressed the same philosophy of innovation and ecology from the perspective of a business person. It became clear to me that this philosophy was like a wave flowing through many aspects of design and business. Rather than changing to a different field, I simply needed to change the way I thought about graphic communication.

All of the authors and innovators I mentioned cut their teeth as 1960s progressives. Over the intervening decades they formulated a philosophy that seemed to reconcile the environmentalism of the 60s with the realities of contemporary science and business—and managed to infuse their work with beauty and creativity along the way.

When I cofounded Celery Design Collaborative with two friends in San Francisco in 1997, we modeled the studio after this group of green pioneers. Our goal was to do graphic design that "tastes good and is good for you." For us, the name "celery" evoked a quirky sort of green that was more interested in innovation than guilt. (I should note here that this is my version of history. My mother, a New Orleans native, insists that celery references "the holy trinity of Louisiana cooking"; my business partner Rod DeWeese insists it has something to do with Bloody Mary cocktails.)

We had the good fortune very early on of working with The Natural Step, an influential nonprofit organization that promotes a science-based framework for sustainable development. Many business people have found The Natural Step model helpful as they attempt to steer their organizations toward sustainable operations. When Celery began working with The Natural Step, Paul Hawken was directing the

the NATURAL STEP

organization in the United States. He encouraged us to try out some ambitious eco-innovations, and we learned from both successes and failures. In the process of designing an identity system, brochures, and educational materials, we learned a great deal about sustainability and were able to help one of the thought leaders of this arena. SEE PAGES 61 AND 90.

In the years since then, Celery has done design work for a wide variety of large and small nonprofit organizations. Helping advocacy organizations get their messages out has been a great way for us to learn and gain experience doing green design. Local organizations like the Ecology Center, which promotes recycling and sustainable lifesyles in our hometown of Berkeley, and global organizations like Future 500, which encourages corporations to adopt sustainable practices, have a great deal in common. They all rely on effective communications to achieve their missions. Therefore, they need, and usually appreciate, good design.

Celery got its first big taste of Fortune 500 work when Gil Friend, a green business guru and founder of Natural Logic, invited us to work on Hewlett Packard's first corporate social responsibility (CSR) report. Gil was advising HP on their CSR strategy, and he thought that a fresh design approach would help the cause. We worked very closely with Gil and the team at HP to build a compelling narrative and a set of easy-to-understand information graphics. Our passion about the content came through in the design and helped to elevate the project beyond typical corporate communications. The report was very well received and it helped to establish HP as one of the early leaders of corporate responsibility reporting in the United States. SEE PAGES 98 AND 179.

The project taught us that green design was equally possible at the largest corporations in the world and at small, local nonprofits. That's because design decisions are not made at the scale of the "corporation," they are made at the scale of the person. Doing interesting, innovative work is largely a matter of connecting with people who share your passions. Those people could be anywhere in the world and could be employed by almost any organization. When you peel back the façade of any great design project, you find a group of people, sitting around a table, trying to think through difficult issues and solve communications problems.

Doing interesting, innovative work is largely a matter of connecting with people who share your passions.

DESIGN IS AN AVOCADO

THE LAYERS OF GREEN DESIGN

There are three distinct ways of thinking about a graphic designer's role: designer as manipulator of stuff; designer as message maker; and designer as agent of change.

I like to think of design as a big, ripe avocado. The outer layer of this avocado represents the physical world of paper and print. This is the obvious part of design that we immediately see—the layer of stuff. Yet if we peel back the skin of the avocado, we discover the meat. This is the realm of brand and information. All of that stuff on the exterior really exists in order to convey information and deliver messages.

If we dive still deeper into the design avocado, we find one more layer—the seed at the center. This seed represents the central challenge around which all of the messages and stuff of design revolve: effecting change.

DESIGNER AS MANIPULATOR OF STUFF

The kind of graphic design that I learned about in school is a world of typography and images, paper and ink. It is the descendant of Gutenberg and the Bauhaus. It is essentially a world of stuff. In this world, graphic designers are manipulators of words, creators of image, and specifiers of materials.

Within this conception of graphics, **green design** is a matter of finding and using better physical materials. Designers may research things such as recycled and tree-free papers; or try to find nontoxic inks; or devise folds and structures that result in less waste. When most designers think of green design, these are the common themes.

In the early days of Celery, we immersed ourselves in the world of alternative materials and manufacturing techniques. We collected a library of unusual papers made from bamboo, banana, beer, and a bounty of other materials. We discovered topics outside the typical realm of graphic design, such as biomimicry, biocomposites, and Bucky Fuller. Ten years later, this is still a big part of what we do. We are researching and experimenting on nearly every project we touch.

DESIGNER AS MESSAGE MAKER

Along the way, I have also come to know a different realm of graphic design—one that is not specifically about stuff. In addition to creating physical artifacts (all those booklets, brochures, and banner ads), graphic designers also help clients strategize about how to build strong brands and craft communications that resonate with their target audiences. As such, we are message makers. The messages designers make, the brands we build, and the causes we promote can have impacts far beyond the paper we print on.

Design is **stuff**.

Design is **message**.

Design is **change**.

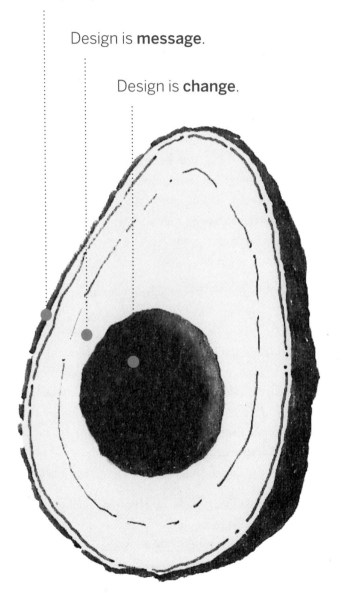

This points to a different level of green graphic design. In addition to seeking out better materials and manufacturing techniques, designers can craft and deliver messages that have a positive impact on the world. An obvious example of this sort of green design is when designers work with nonprofit advocacy organizations. For instance, Celery helps the Global Footprint Network communicate with political leaders around the world about sustainable development. We use green materials, of course, but the ideas and messages we work with have much more potential to change the course of world development than our material choices do.

Likewise, green designers may help values-based companies build strong brands and succeed in the marketplace. These companies in turn help to educate their customers about social and environmental issues. Innovative brands can also have an influence far beyond their market share because they can shift the competitive landscape for major industries. A small company like Elephant Pharmacy, which has four stores in the San Francisco area, has carved out a comfortable niche by focusing on holistic wellness and natural products, but it has also influenced larger competitors to focus more on these things.

However, green messages are not limited to nonprofits and green businesses. Community outreach, cause marketing, and corporate responsibility are all well-developed corporate activities that allow graphic designers to work with messages that can have a positive impact. Designers can help companies position themselves as leaders on social and environmental issues, which in turn can influence business operations for years to come.

DESIGNER AS AGENT OF CHANGE

At its core, design is about effecting change. Someone, somewhere is dissatisfied with the way they find things, and they attempt to improve the situation by investing in design.

As designers, we are trying to help clients change the way people think and/or the way they act. In this sense, designers are uniquely positioned to shift not only our own actions, but also the actions of many others who are touched by our work—including our audiences and our clients. We may be hired to change the user's experience of a client's brand. But in the process of doing this, we have the power to change the brand itself. We have the power to influence the substance of a product or service. Green design at this level is about being a force for positive change.

Your range of possibilities as a green designer is directly related to how you define your role as a designer. If you think of yourself as a manipulator of stuff, then you can specify recycled paper and green printing. If you think of yourself as a message maker, then you can actively help influence the ideas and brands you work with. If you think of yourself as an agent of change, then you just might be able to change the actions of your audience, your clients, and your peers.

GREEN DESIGN IS GOOD DESIGN

Green graphic design is, first and foremost, about using the power of design to shift the status quo toward sustainable solutions.

The past century has witnessed a profound change in the role of graphic designers from a physical craft toward intellectual problem solving—from the factory floor to the cubicles of middle management. In recent years, a handful of design consultancies such as Stone Yamashita Partners and Bruce Mau Design have pointed the way to a future where graphic designers help define long-term corporate strategies and command a place among corporate executives. Many of us still set type and work with printers on production issues, but the **range** of our industry has increased dramatically and will probably continue to increase.

Likewise, the **influence** of graphic design is increasing. As partners with printers, graphic designers influence the flow of enormous quantities of materials and energy. With marketing managers, we influence public opinion and educate customers. With business leaders, we influence the brand value of organizations and help to determine their success or failure.

The power of graphic designers has undoubtedly increased. And with this newfound power comes new responsibility. We have to ask, *Are we having a positive influence, or a negative influence? Is our work making life better for people and for future generations? Or, are we helping to fray the social fabric that holds us together and the ecological systems upon which we all depend?*

Whether our job relates to production, layout, message hierarchy, or brand strategy, all of us can embrace a greener, more responsible model for graphic design. We stand between business and its audience. Just think of the good we could do—if only we choose to use our power!

Green design is a higher order of "good" design. Most of the aesthetic and functional principles that have guided our traditional conception of "good design" still apply. In fact, our work needs to be "good" in order to be green. But green design adds a new set of standards to the old "good design" that encompasses ecological and social "goodness."

As graphic designers, we develop an innate compulsion to fix bad kerning and to clarify muddled messages. That's a big part of "learning to be a designer." It doesn't matter whether it's a major corporate identity system or a toddler's birthday invitation with an audience more likely to eat the design than read it. Most of us are in this field because we enjoy solving visual problems. Over time, we develop an internal compass that guides us and helps us make design decisions.

Yet when it comes to the environmental and social aspects of communications, many designers feel that they need special permission from some higher authority to do the right thing. Suddenly, designers start saying things like *"My boss hasn't asked me to do it"* and *"They're not paying me to be a do-gooder."* But it is **everyone's** job to do good work. If we redefine "good design" to encompass green thinking, then it is automatically part of our job. We don't need permission to do good any more than we need permission to obsess about kerning.

Learning to be a green designer is simply a process of refining that internal compass that guides our design so that it includes social and ecological considerations.

The New York ad agency Green Team developed a tool for assessing the overall "goodness" of communications. They created a web tool, called *After These Messages*, that allows people to view an advertisement, then answer a series of simple questions (*If you created it, would you sleep well at night? Would you put it in your portfolio? Does it contribute to society?*). The tool processes the answers and then plots the ad on a chart with two axes: aesthetic quality (from Hack to Genius) and social benefit (from Heaven to Hell). Anyone is free to make a judgment, and then to see how that compares to the average judgment from all other viewers. It is a fun, often surprising, activity.

After These Messages is a window into the future of design. It is no longer enough to strive for high production values. Designers must also strive for positive social and environmental impact. It is not "good" to be genius if your genius is used to damage society. Our conception of "good design" is changing. After playing with the *After These Messages* tool for a while, all of our design awards programs start to seem shallow and superficial. They seem one-dimensional because they only assess production values, completely ignoring the broader social context. As we adopt a more multidimensional lens for assessing design, green design will become the norm. We all strive to do good design; we just need to update our concept of "good."

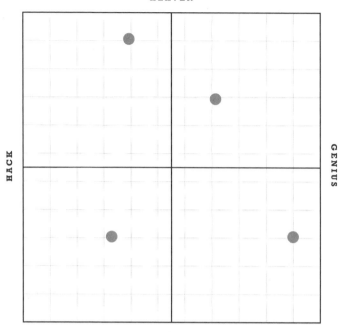

After These Messages is a tool that helps people judge both the aesthetic quality and the social value of advertisements.

©Green Team

THE COMING WAVE

Let's start with a difficult reality: Green design is harder than "normal" design. You will have to learn more, struggle against the status quo, and possibly try things that no one in your organization has tried before. Your boss and/or client won't have the answers for you and may not appreciate your accomplishments. Furthermore, you will probably make some embarrassing and costly mistakes.

Green design, like any change to a well-entrenched status quo, is challenging. The good news is that designers are very good at

overcoming challenges and finding ways to improve upon the past. We are frequently faced with new materials, new tools, new clients, and new audiences to reach. This is what makes graphic design so interesting. For most designers, green issues are just another set of new challenges. The possibilities are exciting, but it won't be easy for any of us to master them.

The important thing to know is this:

Sustainability will define our era.

Human progress never rolls in on wheels of inevitability.

MARTIN LUTHER KING, JR.

Ideas related to sustainability are in the process of transforming the way businesses and other organizations operate and communicate. Sustainability is one of those waves, like the rise of modernism in the 1930s and the personal computer revolution in the 1980s, that change nearly every aspect of our society—and every design industry, including graphic design. We are already seeing the "green" transformation in architecture and industrial design. It doesn't matter what political party you belong to, where you live, how much money you make, or what car you drive. Within the next ten years, almost **every** graphic designer will be a green designer to some degree. The real question is whether you use this shift as an opportunity for growth or allow it to put you at a competitive disadvantage. Whether you surf the wave or allow it to toss you into the rocks.

There are lots of reasons why sustainability is transforming our business. Values branding, corporate responsibility, the realities of ecological overshoot, and the mainstreaming of green are a few of the big ones.

1 VALUES BRANDING. We are moving from an era when consumers made purchasing decisions based primarily on price and performance to an era when consumers make values-based purchasing decisions. Fierce global competition means that nearly every successful product or business quickly spawns multiple copycats. Overseas contract manufacturing means that these competitors often share components and manufacturing techniques, making it even harder to tell them apart. And big-box retail and e-commerce mean that we have access to an almost infinite array of product options. In order to make sense of it all, consumers form "relationships" with companies that are built on trust and a perception of shared values. It is easier for us to "connect" with one of five brands than to compare five hundred competing products.

Meanwhile, mass communications and sophisticated transportation infrastructure have erased many of the regional and socioeconomic differences that defined previous generations. We now assemble into "tribes"—groups of people held together by shared values and interests. "Values branding" is a response to these phenomena. As companies try to connect with particular tribes, they are finding that qualities such as "authenticity" are as important as price and performance. Graphic designers are increasingly being tasked with the challenge of creating this new generation of values-based brands.

2

CORPORATE SOCIAL RESPONSIBILITY. The old model of corporate communications and public relations, built upon control of information and message, is breaking down. Over the past decade, a long string of scandals has taught the public that corporate communications can be an unreliable source for information on the true health of a business. Meanwhile, savvy activist organizations have learned to use grassroots campaigns to spread the word about a wide variety of unsavory activities—despite the best efforts of corporate public relations agencies. We have also seen several high-profile examples of imploding brand value, such as Philip Morris and Enron, which demonstrated to many corporate leaders what can happen when a corporation loses the public's trust.

The result of all this is that many companies are embracing "transparency" and talking a lot more about corporate social responsibility (CSR). The principle of transparency is that companies are better off talking openly about difficult issues and engaging actively with critics, rather than ignoring those issues or hiding behind a façade of corporate marketing and public relations. CSR is an acknowledgment that companies need to do more than make a profit in order to earn the trust, respect, and business of customers. They must answer to the "triple bottom line" of financial, social, and environmental performance. This changes the role of graphic design from something akin to cheerleading to something more like facilitating open dialogue.

3 ECOLOGICAL OVERSHOOT. Few aspects of life in the developed world are currently "sustainable." Population growth and rising rates of material consumption in the developing world make this picture ever more dire. We are, without a doubt, in a state of "ecological overshoot," consuming more resources than the Earth produces on an annual basis and systematically diminishing the Earth's productive systems.

Of course, humans have been doing "unsustainable" things for millennia on a regional level. Occasionally, those unsustainable actions have brought great civilizations to their knees (as documented in Jared Diamond's book *Collapse*). But this is the first time in history that humans have overshot the carrying capacity of ecological systems on a global scale. Global warming is the first ecological crisis that impacts every citizen of every nation on every continent.

Businesses are starting to realize that ecological collapse is bad for business. As Yvon Chouinard, founder of the outdoor clothing company Patagonia, puts it, "There's no profit to be made on a dead planet." That statement applies equally well for graphic designers and their clients. We will need to radically reinvent the way we work in order to operate within very real ecological limits.

4   ECO-QUALITY—THE MAINSTREAMING OF GREEN. It is
nearly impossible to pick up an architecture magazine today
and NOT see something about green design. The business
media issues a steady stream of reports on hot new green
companies and the greening of old industry titans. After a
long courting stage, it seems the world is suddenly in love
with renewable energy. Many of the largest corporations in
the world have made bold public commitments to corporate
responsibility in the past few years and are starting to set
ambitious goals for eco-innovation. In case you hadn't
noticed, green is going mainstream.

Organic food, green building, and renewable energy have all
reached a tipping point. In each of these markets, we have seen
a merger between the mainstream consumer's perception of
"quality" and the idea of "ecological." As a result, consumers
who want the best quality are increasingly attracted to the
ecological solutions. This is a shift from the days when eco-
solutions were marketed as "less bad." Most people don't want
"less bad"; they want good. As Alex Steffen, the founder of
WorldChanging, puts it, "We want affluence without guilt,"
not sacrifice and restriction.

We will continue to see green niches taking significant market share in the mainstream. In response, old-school consumer brands are trying to buy up the niche players and/or reposition themselves as responsible, even revolutionary alternatives. Again, graphic designers have a major role to play in aiding the development of green markets.

Change is coming from many different directions. This is not a fad diet; it is a sea change. The implications for the graphic design industry are profound. And this change will not be easy. Positive change, it seems, always lies uphill. To reach it, we must fight the pull of gravity—the inertia of the status quo. Yet out of need and out of opportunity, the ideas behind the "sustainability era" will transform our industry.

UNDERSTANDING SUSTAINABILITY

The word "sustainable" can apply to any action that does not degrade the systems supporting it, and therefore can persist indefinitely. The systems that support our civilization are the natural systems of the Earth. They provide us with potable water, arable land, temperatures within a certain range, and so forth. Trees grow, fish reproduce, wetlands filter out sewage, rainwater falls and fills the rivers. The cycles continue.

The Earth's systems have a fairly consistent and quantifiable level of productivity. If our collective actions cause us to

"**harvest**" **more resources** during a particular span of time
than the productivity of any of the Earth's systems, then those
actions can be called "unsustainable." If we continue those
actions, we gradually diminish the productivity of the systems.
Overfishing is an obvious example of this. Consuming fresh
water from rivers or underground aquifers at a rate faster than
it is replenished by rain and snow is another example.

If our actions **alter and degrade natural areas**, making them
less productive in the future, then those actions are also

unsustainable. Filling in wetlands to build subdivisions is an example of this. That wetland will never again filter water or incubate aquatic life, so the net productivity of those systems goes down. Another example is clear cutting in forest lands, which can result in erosion of topsoil, making it difficult or impossible for healthy forests to regrow. The eroded soil flows into streams where it can permanently disrupt the spawning of fish. The net result is a degraded natural system. Many people would argue that humans have been altering landscapes for millenia. This is true, but this does not negate the fact that systematic degradation cannot continue indefinitely.

Ecological Footprint by Nation
Each dot represents one million people. The size of each dot is proportional to the per capita ecological footprint for each nation.[1] This map shows the interconnection of population and lifestyle in determining our collective ecological impact.

Also, if our actions produce **materials that accumulate** over time (because they can't be effectively absorbed, decomposed, or filtered by natural systems), then those actions are unsustainable. Persistent chemicals such as dioxins and greenhouse gases are examples of this.

The basic assessment of "sustainability" is a fairly straightforward calculation. Either we are degrading our natural systems or we are not. Either we are producing persistent chemicals or we are not. This assessment of whether or not a particular action is sustainable is not a matter of ethics or opinion. However, what we choose to do, or not do, with the information may indeed be a moral decision.

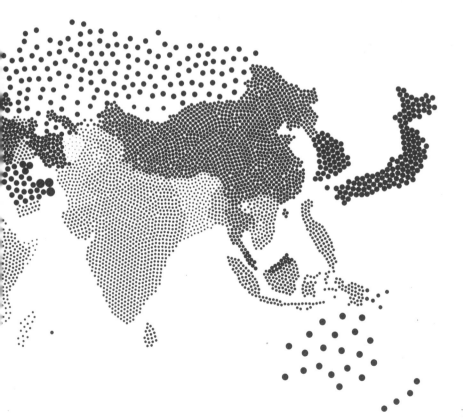

The scientist Mathis Wackernagel, founder of Global Footprint Network, has developed a helpful method for visualizing sustainability with the concept of Ecological Footprints. With the help of other scientists, he calculated the annual productivity for a wide variety of ecological systems, multiplied this by the total area of productive land and sea on Earth, and divided that by the total number of people in each region of the world. The result is an average productivity per acre of land and sea and the per capita productivity of the Earth.[1]

With this in hand, Wackernagel's team is able to translate almost any activity into an area of productive land, or "Ecological Footprint." It is therefore possible to assess whether our resource consumption exceeds the per capita productivity of the Earth.

Since the mid 1980s, the collective resource consumption of humans has exceeded the annual productivity of the Earth. We are in a state that scientists call "ecological overshoot." This means that we are using more resources than our planet can generate.

Through the scientific lens of sustainability, we sometimes see uncomfortable conclusions. Using an ecological footprint calculator,[2] I can calculate the footprint of my personal resource consumption, which comes to about 13 global acres, or 5.2 global hectares. That is less than the average North American (24 acres/person, 9.6 ha/person), but higher than the average

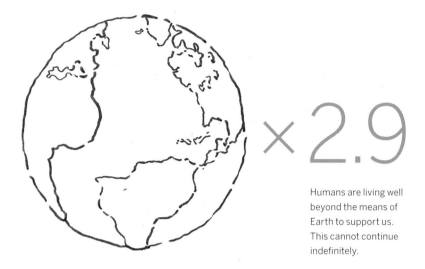

×2.9

Humans are living well
beyond the means of
Earth to support us.
This cannot continue
indefinitely.

German (11.25 acres/person, 4.5 ha/person) and much higher
than the average Earthling (5.5 acres/person, 2.2 ha/person).
More importantly, my Ecological Footprint is significantly
greater than what is available per person—4.5 acres/person,
1.8 ha/person. If everyone lived like me, we would need 2.9
planets to support the world's population indefinitely.
Therefore, MY LIFESTYLE IS NOT SUSTAINABLE.

This puts the whole "paper versus plastic" debate at the grocery
store into perspective. It turns out that both the paper and
the plastic bag are likely to be unsustainable, as are most of the
groceries you're buying and the supermarket you're standing
in while you ponder the question. Perhaps we don't need an
answer to the "paper or plastic" question; we need to design a
different system altogether—a significantly better system.

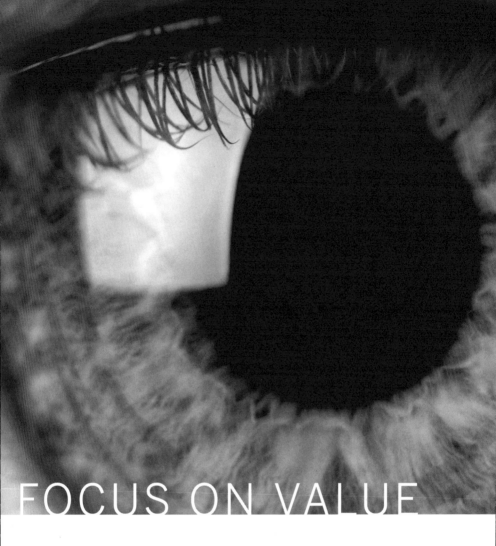

FOCUS ON VALUE

Any designer who wants to tackle ecological issues must face the presumption that alternative materials and manufacturing methods cost too much. It could come from a boss, a peer, or a vendor or from the designer's own conscience—but it certainly will come. There are two problems with that presumption.

First, it is often false. In many cases, it is possible to use environmentally improved materials at the same or lower cost. It may require some research and experimentation, but green design options do not necessarily add cost.

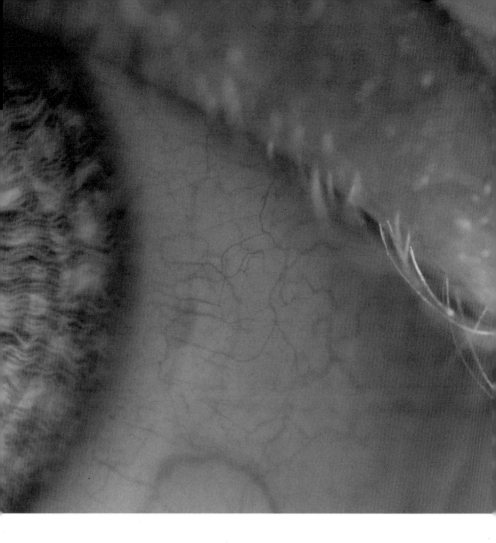

Second, if designers focus only on cost, we may implicitly accept a broken system. Achieving price parity with the status quo may seem like the only viable option, but identifying and fixing major problems with the existing system is often more effective—and may ultimately lead to a cheaper solution. If we take the time to look, we will usually uncover massive levels of waste in the status quo. And changing the system infuses any project with a whole world of creative problem solving and innovation, which is where designers excel.

Managing costs is an important part of everyone's job—designers included. If the cost of something outweighs the value, then we decide that thing is too expensive. Yet that doesn't mean the cheapest option is the best. We all decide to do things (drive a car, buy a house, print a brochure) that are not the cheapest options available to us. We are constantly weighing the cost of an option against its value. And sometimes, added value makes more expensive options the best choice for a situation. The value outweighs the cost.

Imagine, for instance, a typical direct mail project. Let's assume you've been asked to design a small self-mailer brochure with a 15,000 unit print run. The first idea that springs to mind if you want this project to be more "green" is to specify recycled paper. That is a good start. If you do a bit of research, you should be able to find several workable options that contain at least 50 percent post-consumer recycled (PCR) fiber. SEE PAGE 192. It is usually possible to specify 100 percent PCR paper. Another option would be a paper that combines recycled fiber and sustainably harvested virgin fiber certified by the Forest Stewardship Council (FSC) or even an alternative fiber. If you are in a region of North America that enjoys good distribution of alternative papers, your printer may already be using papers like these. If not, you might need to do some extra research to find the proper distributor and connect them with your printer.

Depending on what paper your client customarily uses for printing, you may find that all of the greenest options cost more. At this point, the focus has been solely on materials and costs. If you stop there, the greener options will often lose out. But dig a bit deeper and you discover a whole range of other possibilities.

COST : VALUE

CUTTING COSTS IS NOT THE ONLY OPTION

Designers can make green solutions viable by adding value through innovation.

For a direct mail campaign, one obvious place to look for savings is the mailing list. It is worth asking the marketing team how "clean" the list is and how well targeted it is. By getting rid of addresses that are out-of-date and people who have not responded after multiple mailings, it may be possible to develop a list of 13,000 or even 10,000 addresses that gets the same response as the former list of 15,000. Aside from reducing waste, the savings in printing and postage could easily finance a greener paper selection.

You may also find savings by optimizing your designs to reduce postage costs or to print more efficiently. These are all important, but this is not where the big savings lie. The average direct mail response rate is around 2.6 percent. Three percent is considered very good response. So marketers look at that mailing of 15,000 and say, "*We're hoping to generate 390 new customers.*" What they don't usually acknowledge is, "*We're expecting to waste 14,610 pieces of mail.*"

But designers can look to that 97.4 percent as a huge untapped resource. We can search for innovative ways to change the user's experience, increase response rates, reduce waste, and potentially save the client money—all at the same time.

The current system presumes enormous levels of waste and is often not very effective. The brochures that go straight to the rubbish bin do not drive audience inquiries or build brand value. These are nonessential material flows. We are paying for them, but they don't directly benefit the profitability of our client's business. So what strategies might put a big dent in the portion of our design that is currently going to waste? Could

Ineffective design is waste.

97.4%

WASTE

2.6%

RESPONSE

we better engage the user? Or educate them? Could we add a lot more value to the user's experience so that far fewer people ignore our messages?

In order to fix the system, we need to shift the conversation from material cost to total project value. Once we start looking at the 97.4 percent presumed waste and developing ideas that may significantly increase response rates, the idea of recycled paper being too expensive starts to seem absurd. Paper represents a tiny fraction of our total expenditure, but an important part of our environmental footprint. Rather than quibble about the cost of greener paper, we should apply our creativity to a real challenge—such as *"How do we increase the effectiveness of our designs by a factor of ten?"*

The truth is, innovation may cost more than the status quo. It requires fresh thinking, experimentation, and research. Yet, after weighing the options, most people would acknowledge that innovation pays dividend—the added value outweighs any added cost.

The good news for designers is that adding value is a creative process. Designers are good at adding value. When we focus our creativity on reducing waste, we find novel ways of doing things. We start designing for change.

THE BEAUTIFUL PIG

WHEN EFFICIENCY IS BAD
AND WASTE IS GOOD

Given the inefficiencies in our current communications system, the obvious course of action for any thoughtful designer is to look for ways to improve upon the status quo. This book addresses many aspects of the system and offers suggestions for improvements. However, we should mention two important notes of caution:

1 EFFICIENCY CAN DECEIVE US. Efficiency tells us little or nothing about social benefit or long-term sustainability. Making a system more efficient does not make it socially just or ecologically sustainable. Efficiency is often equivalent to putting lipstick on a pig—it may be pretty, but it's still a pig. As architect William McDonough points out, the gas chambers of Nazi Germany were efficient, but that does not make them good for society. Efficiency is essentially amoral, and it is deceptive to confuse efficiency with goodness.

Also, efficiency claims are often relative claims (such as 20 percent fewer VOCs), which tell us nothing about the effectiveness of the broader system. Slightly less bad is not the same as good. Relative claims are easily manipulated and must be considered with skepticism. Absolute claims, such as the nutrition and ingredient labels on food products, are much more reliable and informative. SEE PAGE 65.

2 WASTE IS NOT NECESSARILY BAD. In a pure business
sense, waste is any output that doesn't add value for an
organization. So all of the trimmings, misprints, and truck
exhaust associated with graphic design are waste. But so are
the brochures that sit unused in warehouses as well as the
advertisements, promos, and swatch books that fail to drive
sales or change audience perceptions.

Waste is only "unsustainable" if it is not part of any natural
cycle or commercial supply chain and therefore accumulates
in the environment. That goes for natural waste and human-
made waste. Truck exhaust is bad because no one has figured
out how to capture and transform it for a profit as product.
Therefore, it spews into the air and accumulates over our cities.
Dioxin likewise accumulates in the tissue of fish and in mother's
milk. Our household garbage accumulates in landfills and can
leach chemicals into groundwater supplies.

However, as any parasitic organism will tell you, one person's
waste could be another person's product. We are all part of a
network of inputs and outputs, product and waste. If we find
productive uses for underutilized outputs, then we transform
those outputs from waste to product. The act of consciously
looking for these types of linkages is called **industrial ecology**.

One of the ways that designers can improve the efficiency of our communications system is by finding productive uses for waste streams. Rather than limiting ourselves to standard materials for designs, we might also look to cast-offs from other industries. These unconventional materials could spur creative solutions—and we might even get them for free. SEE PAGES 56 AND 60.

Studio eg designed brochures for the **Ecowork** furniture line and printed them on obsolete blueprints that were salvaged from local planning departments and architectural firms.

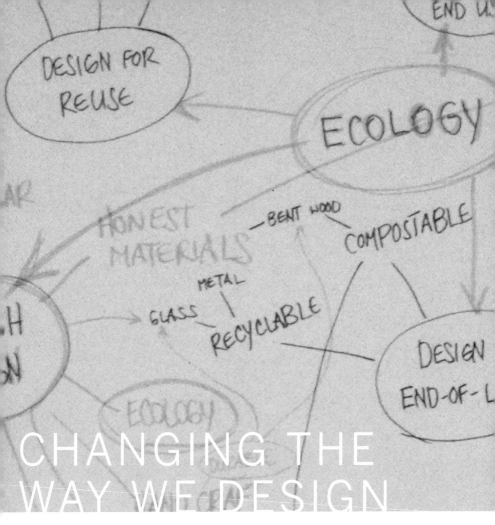

CHANGING THE
WAY WE DESIGN

Most communications systems have so much waste that designers could choose almost any part of that system and quickly imagine ways to make the system more effective. Sounds easy, right?

The problem is that whenever designers try to do anything out of the ordinary in the real world, we encounter roadblocks. Just think of all the excuses from every part of the communications system that might stop you from doing green design right now:

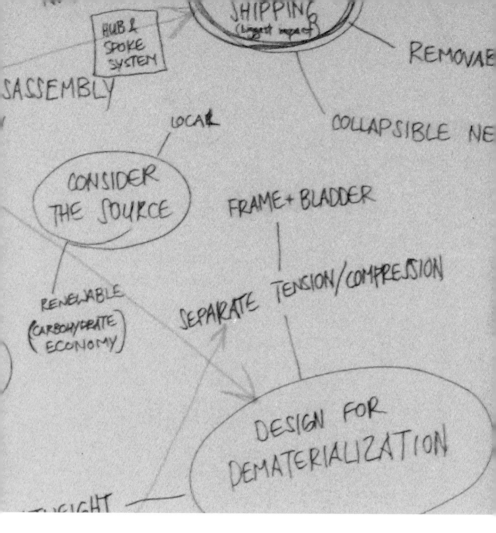

"The customer isn't demanding it."
"It's not in the budget."
"We don't have time."
"There's too much text."
"The printer can't do that."
"That paper is too expensive."

These roadblocks are very real and can be VERY frustrating. In many ways, our success as green designers is defined by how effectively we learn to get past these roadblocks. The good news is that all of these challenges are surmountable. We simply need to look more closely at the roadblocks, figure out where they come from, and develop strategies to help us avoid them.

In order to design for change, we need to change the way we design. Green graphic design attempts to answer the call of our global environmental crisis with innovation and creativity. We search for ways to use far less stuff and to use stuff with a much smaller ecological footprint. We also search for ways to use graphic design as a medium for generating a net benefit in society. This leads to rethinking the role graphic designers play in the communications landscape and refining the traditional range of activities dealing with paper, print, type, image, and story.

We advocate that green designers actively engage with people both **upstream** (relating to business strategy and marketing plans) and **downstream** (relating to materials, manufacturing, and distribution) from the traditional designer's area of expertise. A graphic designer's involvement traditionally lies somewhere between marketing and production. Yet by the time a marketing manager hands off a project plan to a designer, many important decisions that may tie the designer's hands are already made. Likewise, if we release files to production without a great deal of forethought, then our best intentions may never be realized. If we remain in the traditional designer's role, then we limit our potential to have a positive impact. A **whole-system approach** to design is the most effective technique for avoiding the roadblocks that stand in the way of eco-innovation. It also allows designers to see sustainability as a vehicle for innovation and progress, not just a list of restrictions and limitations on our freedom.

Roadblocks for the designer come from both upstream and downstream. The major goal of engaging upstream from the traditional designer's role is to shift the focus of green design from a battle over cost to a strategic conversation about value. By collaborating with our clients and reframing projects in this way, we find that many roadblocks simply disappear. Rather than fight with every little element of the status quo, we try to change the context so that the status quo no longer holds sway. Green design can often perform well on the cost side of the equation, but adding value is the most persuasive means for winning over skeptical clients.

Downstream from design is a long series of stages, as paper manufacturers deliver goods to printers, who hand them off to bindery houses, who then deliver goods to distribution centers, and so on. When we try to insert ecological consider-ations into this mix, we often hear a chorus of *"That's not my job"* or *"My hands are tied"* from people involved in production and distribution. And the truth is that those people are often right. By the time a project gets into production, its destiny is pretty much determined. The only way to change the system is for designers to think creatively ahead of time.

So, rather than handing files to a printer and hoping for the best, a green designer tries to visualize every downstream phase and searches for ways to optimize and innovate.

DESIGNING BACKWARDS

"Designing backwards" is a process by which designers take a mental journey, starting from a design project's ultimate destination and working backwards until we arrive back at the design studio. It's a multiphase brainstorm process, really. Along the way, designers gain knowledge that informs the choices we make. That knowledge enables us to creatively avoid most of the roadblocks that might prevent green solutions from continuing downstream.

6 WASTE

Design for destiny;
Consider reuse;
Recyclability;
Compostability

5 USER

User experience;
Add value through
design; Educate;
Enable action

4 DELIVERY

Design for distribution;
Explore efficient packing;
Stripping away layers;
Alternative distribution

Start at the end, by imagining the best possible destiny for a design. Next, imagine the user's experience with the design and envision scenarios that would make the experience particularly memorable or valuable. Visualize the process for distribution and delivery to the user, including warehousing, packaging, and transport. Search for methods that would be more efficient and effective than the status quo. Finally, define a greenest-case scenario for how the design could be printed, bound, and finished. This includes all of the materials that go into the manufacturing and the ecological impacts of the manufacturing process itself.

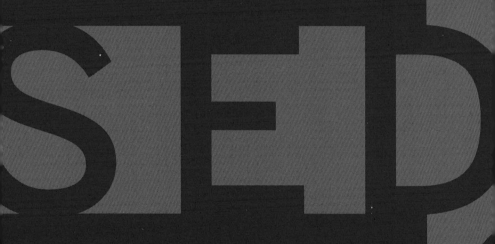

3 WAREHOUSE

Consider print on demand;
Perform actual usage audit

2 BINDERY

Consider mechanical
bindings; Eliminate
trim waste

1 PRINTING

Design for green printing;
Explore recycled paper;
Design press sheets;
Consider digital printing;
UV inks; Low VOC printing

THE END

DESIGN FOR DESTINY

The starting point for our backwards journey is "the end."
In most cases, graphic design projects end here in a landfill …

GREEN GRAPHIC DESIGN

… or if we're lucky, here in a recycling facility.

It's hard to imagine during the excitement of brainstorming and layout, but that beautiful design you're working on will end up as trash. It will be thrown away.

But "away" is not really a destiny. It is usually a euphemism for burying something in a hole and covering it with dirt. There is a simple fact of planetary life—nothing goes away. For all practical purposes, we live in a sealed container, allowing only light to enter and heat to escape. We are on what Buckminster Fuller called "Spaceship Earth," sealed up tightly and hurtling through space. With very few exceptions, all of our design output will stay onboard indefinitely.

DESTINIES FOR DESIGN MATERIALS

That means all of the paper, plastics, glues, inks, foils, coatings, and other finishes that make up our designs eventually go somewhere, and that somewhere is not so far away. There are six potential destinies for the materials graphic designers specify:

1. PERPETUAL LITTER
   for plastics and other persistent materials lingering in the ocean or on land

2. LANDFILL
   either conventional or hazardous waste

3. INCINERATION
   converting materials into energy + air emissions + ash

4. COMPOST
   through a municipal program or at home

5. RECYCLING
   into reusable fiber, polymers, or metals

6. REUSE
   for the same or a different purpose

It is possible to look at each of these destinies through the lens of material value. Each represents a loss of material value (with the possible exception of fully reusable designs). Yet some destinies are better than others.

PERPETUAL LITTER is the truly worst destiny for the materials we design. This is particularly a problem for plastics waste. In places without sophisticated waste disposal infrastructure, plastic trash has become a permanent pox on the natural landscape. Meanwhile, ocean currents have assembled plastic trash into several massive "garbage patches" of floating debris covering an area twice the size of Texas out in the middle of the Pacific Ocean.[3]

LANDFILL is an ecological dead end, although a somewhat "managed" dead end. Materials that end up there essentially have no value for society or for the natural ecosystem. Worse still are materials that require a **hazardous waste** landfill. These materials demand special treatment, often at great expense, to protect society and the natural environment from their inherent toxicity. The first thing to do when we design for destiny is to eliminate materials that require hazardous waste handling. Later in this book we'll identify some of those materials and propose strategies for avoiding them.

SEE CELERY'S SUSTAINABILITY SCORECARD, PAGES 63 AND 186.

INCINERATION is the end of the line for material structure, but some of the energy embodied in the material can be captured and put to good use. Aside from energy, there are two main outputs from incineration, gaseous emissions and solid ash, and each can be problematic. Some materials, such as polyvinyl chloride (PVC) plastics, release hazardous gases if they are burned. Other materials, such as the metallic pigments in some inks, end up concentrated in the solid ash remaining after waste is burned. While the concentration levels in the initial use may be considered nontoxic, they can result in toxic incineration ash that must be handled as hazardous waste. The material choices that designers make have a direct impact on how good or bad incineration is for society and the natural world.

COMPOSTING represents a complete loss of physical structure, but the nutrients embodied in the materials continue to circulate within our ecosystem. They might serve to fertilize food crops or provide habitat for important microorganisms. As with incineration, though, the devil is in the details. A biodegradable polymer bag printed with noncompostable inks or a piece of compostable paper coated with a plastic laminate is essentially contaminated. Celery has a compost bin in the courtyard of our studio, and we see the results of bad material choices every time we turn the soil. For years, we've been composting food scraps and paper "to go" cups and containers. The paper from these containers would decompose, leaving behind an annoying plastic laminate which we would have to filter out of the compost by hand. Our local grocery chain eventually got smart (or at least reacted to customer complaints) and switched to fully biodegradable containers.

RECYCLING maintains far more of a material's value. Some metals and polymers can be recycled indefinitely with little or no loss of structure. In these cases, the recycled material is "as good as new." Other materials, such as paper and most plastic, lose some structural quality or purity when they are recycled. This is sometimes called "downcycling" because, for instance, the paper fibers get broken and are weaker than virgin fibers. Yet a great deal of material value is maintained. Any coatings and inks applied to a material must be removed during the recycling process. For metals and many plastics, this happens when the material is melted down. For paper, it happens through a "de-inking" process. A big part of designing for recyclability is eliminating or isolating any add-on materials that contaminate the base material and make it more difficult to recycle.

Recycling usually entails melting, pulping, shredding, or otherwise reconstituting a material, but that's not always necessary. Many materials maintain enough structural integrity to be reprocessed or, better yet, recontextualized. Designers can look to waste streams as a source for inexpensive alternative materials that often have a built-in back-story.

Celery created the cover of the **Thinkbook** journal from recycled silicone rubber sheets. The rubber had previously been used in an industrial process for stamping computer wires. This process left the material with an interesting ridged texture—like slick, space-age corduroy. Silicone is an inherently "nonstick" material, so conventional printing and bindery would not adhere well to it. Instead, we die-cut typography on the cover and designed a unique mechanical binding system. Individual paper sections are saddle-stitched with "loop" staples, then the sections and the cover are held together with rubber straps. The binding system is specially designed so that the interior sections can be removed and replaced, which allows the cover to be used for many years.

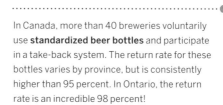

REUSE is the highest order of "design for destiny" because it represents the greatest persistence of material value. If a design is used twice instead of just once, its ecological footprint for the function performed could easily drop by half. If it is used several times, the ecological impact drops to a mere fraction. That dividing effect makes the reusable design more efficient than the single-use design in many situations.

There are many different flavors of design for reuse:

In Canada, more than 40 breweries voluntarily use **standardized beer bottles** and participate in a take-back system. The return rate for these bottles varies by province, but is consistently higher than 95 percent. In Ontario, the return rate is an incredible 98 percent!

According to Jeff Newton of Canada's National Brewers Association, "The bottle is reused/refilled an average of 15 times before being crushed and recycled into a new bottle. Hence you can use one bottle to do the work of 15 thus avoiding the manufacture and resource depletion associated with manufacturing 15 separate one-way bottles. Not only is this good for the environment but it helps brewers lower their costs of purchasing new bottles—buy one bottle and use it 15 times versus buy 15 bottles and use them once."

NetFlix uses returnable mailing envelopes, which drastically reduce the amount of paper required for customers to mail back rented DVDs. The company has mailed over one billion DVDs since its founding, so the ecological implications of that design decision are staggering. FedEx uses a returnable envelope design that allows customers to mail their monthly payments in the same envelope that contained their bill. The company Ecoenvelopes markets a similar envelope system to other companies in North America. In the United Kingdom, **Shuttlepost** markets a line of durable plastic envelopes that are reusable many times.

Aveda designed a reusable tube container for lipstick, made of aluminum and a biocomposite material. After their initial purchase, customers can save money and avoid waste by purchasing make-up inserts that fit into the reusable tube. Aveda projects that each tube could be used twelve times before disposal.

TerraCycle is a New Jersey start-up that markets garden fertilizer made from food scraps. The liquid fertilizer is packaged in reused plastic soda bottles. In order to procure a steady source of usable bottles, TerraCycle sponsors bottle collection drives at elementary schools—a smart strategy that keeps bottles out of the waste stream and also engages parents and kids with the TerraCycle brand.

©Turner & Associates

In 1999, Celery designed a reusable annual report for **The Natural Step**. The report was written as a series of detachable postcards, and each card included a message for readers to "Tell a Friend" by mailing the card. The strategy was to promote a "viral effect" whereby readers could become promoters. Turner & Associates designed an annual report for **Yahoo** in 1999 that also included reusable postcards.

A FRAMEWORK WITH A FUTURE...

The Natural Step is a non-profit environmental organization helping businesses, communities and other groups redesign their activities to become more sustainable. TNS provides a framework that is based on science and serves as a compass to guide decision-making. To learn more, please visit our web site at **www.naturalstep.org** or call (415) 561-3344.

the NATURAL STEP

TELL A FRIEND! Help spread the word about The Natural Step by sending this card to someone you know. Printed on 100% post-consumer recycled paper with soy inks.

THE SUSTAINABILITY SCORECARD

Graphic designers could argue that the destiny of our design work depends upon the actions of consumers and government officials in cities where the designs end up. Designers can't control whether a customer tosses a brochure in the trash or whether a city provides curbside recycling bins. However, the range of potential destinies for our work is often strictly limited before it reaches the end user. The moment a designer specifies a plastic laminate or a vinyl banner, the destiny of that design is pretty well set: It will end up in a landfill.

Our job as green designers is to enable **the best possible destiny** for our work. We can't know what others will do, but we can do our part by creating designs that won't **necessarily** end up in a landfill. We do this by choosing appropriate materials and by avoiding contaminants during production.

At Celery, we use a simple "Green, Yellow, Red" system for quickly assessing materials—we call it our sustainability score-card. We look at three factors: SOURCE, ENERGY, and DESTINY, and rank the range of available options from best to worst.

This system is not a replacement for doing thorough research and making case-by-case decisions based on individual circumstances. Most materials get a mixed score, which forces us to weigh the factors against one another. But the system serves as a quick and easy starting point for deciding what materials to specify.

We based our system on the Sustainability Toolkit and Score card developed by Michael S. Brown, PhD, for the catalog retailer Norm Thompson Outfitters. Brown, a specialist in environmental assessment, created the original tool to help professional buyers quickly assess the relative merits of products they were considering for inclusion in the Norm Thompson catalog. Buyers were given up to three points for a solidly "green" product and negative three points for a thoroughly "red" product. Buyers were challenged to achieve their sales goals while also maximizing their points on the Sustainability Scorecard. This tool teaches buyers and also creates a competitive environment where buyers are recognized and rewarded for minimizing ecological impact.

Celery applied the same strategy to graphic design and created a simple tool that helps us decide which materials to use and which to avoid. It doesn't necessarily make the decisions easy, but it provides a framework for problem-solving and helps us identify how best to allocate limited resources of research time and money. SEE PAGE 186 FOR A COMPLETE SCORECARD.

	SOURCE	ENERGY IMPACTS	DESTINY
PREFERRED +	Made from sustainably harvested, renewable resource; no known toxicity	Made with renewable energy; very moderate embodied energy	Fully recyclable; fully compostable; reusable
CAUTION	Made from conventional renewable resource	Made with nonrenewable energy; low embodied energy	Compatible with incineration
AVOID	Made from nonrenewable resource; known toxic impacts	Made with nonrenewable energy; high embodied energy	Requires conventional or hazardous waste landfill

STANDARDS &
ALPHABET SOUP

Nearly all of the environmental claims in the graphic arts industry relate to process improvements and waste-reducing measures at **particular phases** of production. The result is an alphabet soup of acronyms and competing environmental claims. There are post-consumer and pre-consumer recycled fibers, ECF, TCF, FSC, UV ink, soy inks, and so on. It is very difficult to discern what all of these mean, and which ones represent significant improvements. SEE THE GLOSSARY ON PAGE 189 FOR SOME HELP. One problem is that all of these environmental claims focus on specific links of the chain and tell us almost nothing about the effectiveness of the overall system.

What we need is an integrated system that rolls up the whole system of inputs and outputs into an easy-to-understand meta standard. The standard needs to present concrete, verifiable information and should be structured so that the highest level of achievement requires a major shift from the status quo. This might be an evolution of the Forest Stewardship Council's Chain of Custody standard, or some sort of LEED rating system for graphic arts. (LEED is the U.S. Green Building Council's Leadership in Energy and Environmental Design rating system for high-performance green buildings.) SEE PAGE 129. The standard would need to address a wide range of impacts, but must be simple to understand.

A standard like this would enable companies to easily write substantive environmental standards into their procurement requirements. The result could be a rapid shift in the industry as the chaos of competing claims gives way to an organized "race to the top" with competitors trying to out-green one another.

It's one thing for a company like Coca-Cola to promote some new LEED-certified building it has built, but Coke is not really in the construction business. Imagine if Coke was to adopt some sort of open "green packaging" standard for its billions of containers and "green advertising" standards for its marketing materials. This would be much more closely tied to Coke's core business and brand—and have a much more significant environmetal benefit.

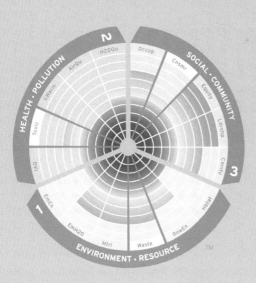

Two proposed systems for judging products and materials in a holistic way: **The Pharos Project** developed for building materials; and the **Eco Nutrition Label**, proposed by industrial designer Jeremy Faludi for consumer goods.

IMPACT

USER EXPERIENCE & TARGETING

The next stop in our "designing backwards" journey—just before the end—is the moment when a member of the audience interacts with our work. The desired outcome of this interaction is some change in belief or behavior. Those changes drive sales, build brand value, and help determine the success or failure of the client's business.

It is fairly standard practice for graphic designers to think about the user when we design, to clearly define objectives, and even to talk about "success metrics." But, as an industry,

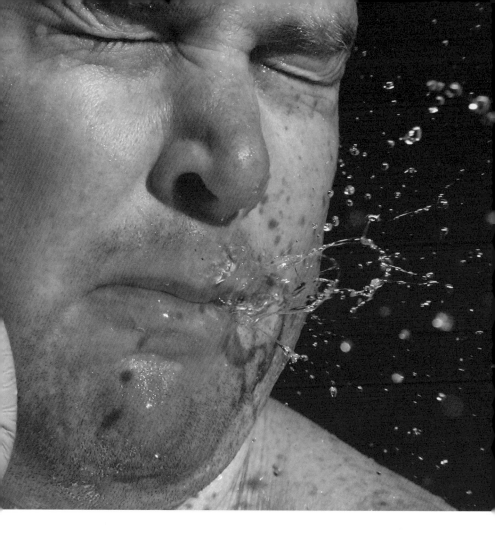

graphic designers tend to be pretty lax in how we analyze the effectiveness of our work in **actually delivering the desired action**. We could learn a lot from the targeting and audience tracking performed by marketers and the human factors scenario planning performed by industrial designers.

There are both financial and ecological reasons for graphic designers to focus more on strategies for effectiveness. If our work were more effective, we could use far less stuff to achieve the desired outcome, which would save money and reduce environmental impacts. **Good design is greener than bad design** because it actually achieves desired outcomes without blanketing the world with poorly conceived, poorly executed communications. Increasing our response rates is one of the greenest things we can do as designers.

Incremental improvements are good, but we're also looking for paradigm-shifting design solutions, which can generate enormous audience "buzz" and therefore may be far more effective than typical solutions.

UNDERSTANDING USERS

Human factors specialists work with industrial designers to focus on the physical and psychological aspects of a user's experience with using products and performing tasks. They observe users in their home and work environments and try to discover patterns of use or places where products don't serve their intended purposes. These observations often spur product ideas and refinements and sensitize designers to the needs of the user. Designers build quick mock-ups and work through role-playing scenarios before refining the product and dealing with aesthetics, functionality, and styling. Ideally, the result is a product that is both desirable and intuitively usable.

Human factors specialists also work with user interface designers to develop Web sites. Designing a good user interface is a matter of predicting user behavior and providing an intuitive path to accomplish tasks. A user's **natural** action should be the **correct** action. Again, the process begins with quick "wire frame" mock-ups and scenario plans, which inform the finished design.

Designers focus on the user experience and eliminate unnecessary information in order to build an intuitive, elegant interface (like Apple's iPod or Google's online calendar tool).

A human factors approach can also make other graphic design projects more effective. It helps designers visualize and optimize the user experience for any design project. A small example of this approach is a project that Celery designed for the national AIGA office.

We were asked to create a logo and certificate for CarbonCool, a program that allows graphic designers and studios to offset their greenhouse gas emissions. As we began designing the certificate, we identified two points of use: when someone at the AIGA office prints a participant's name on the certificate and mails it to the recipient, and when the recipient displays the certificate in their office. We ran through some simple scenarios on each point of use and came up with several conclusions:

- The certificate paper should be heavyweight, but must be laser printer compatible.

- It should be a standard 8½"×11" so that it fits into a standard paper tray.

- In order for the certificate to be mailed undamaged, it requires a rigid backer.

- Recipients will either display it in a frame or prop it on a shelf.

- It is less expensive and uses less stuff to display the certificate unframed, but this would require a rigid backer and some sort of easel.

This information drove our paper choice, of course. We chose the heaviest laser-guaranteed paper we could find that was made with a high percentage of recycled fiber (Domtar Earthchoice Proterra, 40 percent post-consumer recycled, 80lb. cover). The user scenarios also influenced our overall design. We created an 8½"× 11" certificate and also designed a chipboard backer that does double duty as a mailing stiffener and an easel for display. We also designed a custom mailing envelope made from the printer's make-ready scrap so that the user's experience with the piece begins at the moment they pick up their mail.

The **AIGA CarbonCool** certificate features an integrated easel for shipping and display.

A certificate like this is sent out after the point of sale, so some might argue that we should do the cheapest solution possible to minimize cost. We considered doing a PDF certificate that participants could print on their own, at no cost to the AIGA. Yet after looking at the full scenario, we decided that a positive experience and a compelling "story" would encourage participants to talk about the program and increase the chance of generating media buzz. We determined that the CarbonCool program was more likely to succeed if we did something interesting than if we just did something cheap. We felt that the environmental benefit of a successful campaign would outweigh the environmental impact of printing the certificates.

This small, simple project demonstrates the potential of user scenario planning. This is a narrative method that helps designers understand their audience better, enabling us to create designs with which the audience is more likely to interact.

This is a narrative method that helps designers understand their audience better, enabling us to create designs with which the audience is more likely to interact.

Another example is the packaging system that design consulting company IDEO created for Pangea Organics. The design team took a holistic approach to the packaging project. In addition to using containers with high amounts of post-consumer plastic and doing away with most of the paper labels, the designers found innovative ways to engage users with the package. Instead of a standard paperboard box, the Pangea boxes are made of molded paper pulp that is infused with wildflower seeds. Users are invited to soak the box in water then plant it in their garden. With regular watering and a little luck, the "trash" will become a beautiful flower patch. This design concept is a direct outcome of a human factors approach to design. By focusing on the user's experience, designers can devise radical solutions that are still easy to use and compelling for their audience.

Pangea Organics packaging was designed to engage the user in a memorable experience— of growing wildflowers.

TARGETING

One reason that typical graphic design and marketing response rates are low is that "the Audience" and "the Project" are often seen as monolithic units. The definition of audience that graphic designers use is usually vague and not very helpful during the creative process. Meanwhile, direct mail marketers have become much more sophisticated in how they define and target subsets of the overall audience. How can graphic designers learn from this and apply that knowledge to make a broad array of communications materials more efficient?

There are two sides to audience targeting: the research side and the design side. The goal of research is to break up the monolithic audience population into smaller groups that share certain beliefs or traits. Market researchers define "affinity groups" based on age, values, purchasing habits, geography, or any number of other factors. Designers and copy writers take information from the research phase and tailor communications specifically for each affinity group. When it works well, the result is personalized to audience interests and far more effective than one-size-fits-all communication. In very simple

©IDEO

terms, an audience segmentation exercise can force designers to think about precisely whom they are trying to communicate with—and what those people are likely to respond to. For instance, when we start an annual report project, we may segment the audience into groups on the basis of how they typically read reports:

Skimmers read introductory paragraphs, pull quotes, and photo captions. They are looking for performance trends and the "big picture" on strategy.

Analysts are mainly interested in data, statistics, and policies.

Subject area enthusiasts want an interesting narrative about a specific topic.

These types of audience segments help us design multiple paths of navigation through the report contents. If we plan ahead, we can create a single communications piece that is equally engaging for skimmers, analysts, and subject area enthusiasts. Vague audience designations such as "employees" and "shareholders" are less likely to influence the form and function of a design than a clear understanding of the different ways that it will be used.

Another trick of the direct marketing trade is **variable data printing**. This is the technology behind all the junk mail you get with your name on a fake credit card. Despite its cheesy reputation, variable data printing is not incompatible with great design, and it is a powerful tool for targeting communications. The designer can designate variable areas of text or image in a layout and swap content for those areas instantaneously. The designer can then control what content each audience group gets. A digital press pulls the variable content from a database, merges it into the layout, and creates the appropriate number of prints.

Designers need not be content with the gimmick of printing a reader's name on a brochure. Imagine a university newsletter that is tailored to the interests of each reader. Perhaps each reader gets five articles, assembled from a pool of twenty articles, selected on the basis of the reader's age, profession, whether he or she has kids, or has donated money to the school, or any number of other variables. The design styles and photos could likewise be variable. Readers would be far more likely to take notice if the styling and EVERY article were tailored for them. What would the response rate on something like that be? Could you double the typical 6–12 percent response rate on university mailings? Of course you could. Perhaps you could quadruple it. A sophisticated variable design campaign may cost several times more to build than a standard monolithic design, but a much higher response rate easily pays for that investment.

COLLECTING AND INTERPRETING FEEDBACK

Calculating response rates can only be done in retrospect. It is impossible to know precisely what will work and what won't work with communications until you try something and observe the results. The same can be said of measuring the ecological efficiency of a project: You can only become more efficient if you know how efficient you were in the past.

The challenge for graphic designers is that we don't have well-developed feedback loops. Whether it is because design studios tend to work on a project-by-project basis or simply because we don't ask for the data, graphic designers typically know very little about what happens with our work when it reaches the intended audience. In order to make our work more effective and more ecologically efficient, we need to continually learn from our mistakes. And we need to create solid benchmark metrics against which we judge success.

Feedback is an essential element in effective green graphic design. It allows for continual improvement, of course, but it also opens the door to a huge pile of FREE MONEY. On many levels, eco-efficiency is a matter of shifting budgets from the waste column to the design column. It is about using more creativity and less stuff. If designers can demonstrate that eco-innovation is budget-neutral or that it improves the client's bottom line, then many of the roadblocks preventing innovation simply fall away. When designers can demonstrate that eco-innovation actually improves top-line performance, increases response rates, or gains market share, they can gain access to the magical HOV lane to design success. But designers can't demonstrate anything in these terms without measurable data and continuous feedback on the performance of our work.

Pamela Fogg is the art director at Middlebury College in Vermont. Over the past five years, she and a small team of designers have updated the school's brand and shifted all the printed communications materials produced by the school to premium recycled papers. Some of the new papers cost more than their virgin pulp predecessors, but Pam didn't finance the shift by asking for more money. Instead, she began auditing the storage closets where old communications materials go to die. She looked at how many course catalogs, applications, and handbooks were left unused, then adjusted the new print runs in response to that feedback. By eliminating waste, she freed up her budget for better materials. Middlebury's communications are more efficient and have a smaller ecological impact—at no additional cost.

Eco-efficiency is a matter of shifting budgets from the waste column to the design column. It is about using more creativity and less stuff.

Auditing actual performance and collecting data are a great first step. Performance data feedback becomes far more meaningful for determining efficiency if we figure out how to **normalize** the information correctly. For this, we divide a physical impact (i.e., total brochures printed, total greenhouse gas emissions, total water used) by some aspect of business productivity (i.e., total sales, number of new customers, total dollars raised). The result is a measure of "ecological impact per unit of productivity," or ecological efficiency.

The first generation of "eco-audits" for graphic designers, which are promoted by several paper companies, start down the path of normalized metrics. In this case, the paper audits measure the number of trees harvested, pounds of greenhouse gases, gallons of water used, ... **per pound of paper used**. For recycled papers, the eco-audits compare the actual ecological

NEW LEAF PAPER®

ENVIRONMENTAL BENEFITS STATEMENT

of using post-consumer waste fiber vs. virgin fiber

Using 10,000 pounds of New Leaf Reincarnation Matte, made with 100% recycled fiber and 50% post-consumer waste, processed chlorine free, and manufactured with electricity that is offset with Green-e® certified renewable energy certificates saves the following resources:

trees	water	energy	solid waste	greenhouse gases
58	12,657	26	2,769	4,679
fully grown	gallons	million Btu	pounds	pounds

Calculations based on research by Environmental Defense and other members of the Paper Task Force.

©2007 New Leaf Paper   www.newleafpaper.com

New Leaf Paper was one of the first companies to provide customers with an eco-audit for their paper purchases.

impact to presumed impact if you had used virgin paper and deliver the calculation as a measure of "trees saved," "pounds of greenhouse gas avoided," and "gallons of water saved."

The problem with these first-generation eco-audits is that they rarely measure anything that drives the success of the organization buying paper. They measure impacts per pound of paper used, but most organizations are not in the business of using paper. They are in the business of making money, recruiting customers, or educating students. So a more useful metric would be "trees harvested per new customer" or "pounds of greenhouse gas per dollar of sales." Metrics like these provide the necessary feedback for setting substantive targets for reducing ecological impacts over long periods of time.

This allows the graphic designer to become a partner in achieving core business objectives while also reducing the client organization's environmental footprint. Rather than, *How much extra are you willing to spend on paper?*, the conversation becomes, *How could we reduce the greenhouse gas emissions required to get each new customer?* The answer to this challenge could be wasting fewer brochures, using recycled paper, shifting transactions online, or any number of other creative solutions. The answer to the *How much extra are you willing to spend?* question is usually, *Nothing.*

Again, the roadblocks just fall away.

PACKED WITH GOODNESS

DESIGN FOR DISTRIBUTION & PACKAGING

Let's continue on our backwards journey. Before "the end" and before "the user," our design needs to get to where it is going. When we looked at the user's experience, we tried to learn a few tricks from marketers and other designers. This time, we are going to look for lessons from packaging engineers and logistics specialists.

Distribution is an essential part of all printed graphics—and yet something that graphic designers almost never consider.

Even when we are hired to design product packaging, graphic designers tend to think about the surface or the label, not the process of moving stuff from point A to point B. We generally leave that to the specialists. Green graphic designers need to understand a few principles of efficient transport and then actively collaborate with these specialists in order to change the status quo and create ecologically innovative designs.

TYPES OF PACKAGING

Packaging engineers often separate their world into primary and secondary packaging. Primary packaging is the layer closest to the product. Its functions may include identifying a product, protecting it from damage, holding multiple components together, or attracting a buyer's attention. Secondary, teritary and transport packaging typically serves the function of holding multiple products together and protecting them for efficient transport. Secondary packaging is often discarded before a product gets to the end user.Primary and secondary packaging systems may each contain many layers and materials.

For instance, if the product is liquid pasta sauce, the primary package may include a glass jar, a printed paper label with adhesive on back, and a printed metal lid. The secondary packaging may include a corrugated case with printing on the exterior, chip board dividers, and adhesives to seal the box. The secondary and transport packaging system will also probably include wooden pallets, plastic cling wrap, or metal tension straps to hold multiple cases onto the pallets, and even steel shipping containers that contain multiple pallets for transit by truck, train, or ship.

If the "product" is a personal letter, then the primary packaging would be an envelope. In this instance, there would not be any secondary packaging. If the "product" is a corporate brochure that will be handed out by salespeople, then the secondary packaging may be plastic shrink wrap for sets of 100 brochures, corrugated boxes to hold multiple sets, and plastic bubble wrap to fill dead air space in the box. In this instance, there would not be any primary packaging.

There is no one–size–fits–all solution for sustainable packaging, but it is possible to identify some key principles of successful systems. Sustainable packaging systems tend to fall into two basic categories: the ephemeral and the durable.

Ephemeral packaging is lightweight and biodegradable. It is designed to last as long as necessary and not much longer. Ephemeral packaging fits comfortably into universally available cycles of recycling and regeneration by way of composting.

In the United Kingdom, a company called Greenbottle has developed an interesting ephemeral packaging solution that is a more sustainable alternative to the HDPE plastic milk jug. The unique container is composed of two parts: an outer shell made from recycled paper pulp and a thin, flexible liner made from a corn-based biopolymer. The shell gives the package rigidity; the liner holds the liquid in and keeps it from spoiling. The two parts are easily separable so that customers can recycle the paper shell and compost the liner.

The U.S. Postal Service worked with eBay and McDonough Braungart Design Chemistry to develop a truly ephemeral packaging solution for Express Mail delivery. The new package is "Cradle to Cradle" certified, meaning that every aspect of the system is compatible with either natural nutrient cycles (through composting) or industrial recycling systems. The design of the box didn't change, but the manufacturing process was thoroughly vetted.

Durable packaging strives for many functional lives prior to being discarded. In order to be successful, the package needs to have a strong persistence of value so that people want to interact with it again and again over a long period of time. Durable packaging systems either require industry standardization, so that many manufacturers can share a centralized collection system or tightly controlled cycles of distribution and collection. SEE PAGE 58.

Straus Family Creamery in Northern California has developed an effective durable packaging solution for its organic milk products. The milk is sold in glass bottles, which require a $1.25 deposit. This is, of course, a throw-back to the milkman distribution systems of yesteryear. In addition to avoiding many tons of plastic waste over the years, the bottles have been a fantastic brand differentiator for Straus, building name recognition and customer loyalty. The system works for a number of reasons. Straus sells a premium, organic product, and its target customers are willing to pay a premium for something that they perceive as being environmentally friendly. Also, retailers have agreed to collect the deposit on each bottle and the used bottles that customers bring back to the store. The average bottle is reused eight times and the return rate is about 95 percent.

The Straus Family Creamery system illustrates the importance of a **high persistent value** in durable packaging. The package is unique, high quality, nicely designed, and relatively expensive—all of which encourages people to reuse it. The bottles are heavy and require significant amounts of energy to manufacture, but the company ships its products relatively short distances and has managed to keep tight control over its distribution and collection system, so the bottles get reused many times. Many companies would hesitate to make such a significant investment in design and infrastructure. However, for Straus Family Creamery, the return on that investment has been excellent.

Both ephemeral and durable models offer exciting possibilities for designers. Both also represent a departure from our current design landscape, where our design model is ephemeral and our material choices are often durable.

The durable packaging used by **Straus Family Creamery** is used eight times before being recycled.

An excellent example of ephemeral packaging, the **Greenbottle** is made from recycled paper pulp and a flexible biopolymer bag.

Plastic grocery bags are a common example of mismatched material and usage. Their functional lifespan averages about 10 minutes—holding groceries from the store to a car and from the car trunk to a customer's kitchen. Yet the material (usually polyethylene plastic) will last for thousands of years. Retailers have long laid responsibility on the consumer to recycle these things, yet they have done nothing to develop standardized formulations for manufacturing and universally available recycling systems. It makes no sense to expect customers to clean up a mess made through bad design decisions on the part of manufacturers and retailers.

The City of San Francisco recently took steps to rectify the situation by forcing retailers to use biodegradable plastic or paper bags. In Germany, South Africa, Australia, China, and India, governments have implemented similar programs and usage fees in an attempt to battle the scourge of plastic bags polluting the landscape. Other countries and municipalities will probably follow and finally we may see an end to the false choice of, *paper or plastic?*

As designers, we should not settle for the lesser of two evils. We should invent better solutions that solve functional and aesthetic packaging challenges with materials that are appropriate to their use.

FREIGHT-FRIENDLY DESIGNS

If you are designing a package for mass production, and especially if the packaging you are designing will be shipped long distances, think about how the dimensions of your primary package design impacts the secondary packaging system.

Smart packaging designers look for ways to minimize dead space within the package, within the case, within the pallet, and even within the shipping container. For large companies, the environmental and cost savings can be surprisingly high. The home furnishings giant IKEA has mastered this concept with its assemble-it-yourself furniture.

The easiest way to get rid of dead air is to make packages rectangular and to size them so they fit snugly in a case. But that's not always practical or desirable. It might be more interesting to think about other ways that packages could nest. Trapezoidal shapes can nest well, as can packages with some sort of s-curve. The rectangular Every Man Jack bottle features an offset spout that allows bottles to nest end-to-end.

An offset spout on this bottle allows the product to be nested end-to-end.

REDESIGN BOX GEOMETRY

EXCERPTED FROM THE OREGON DEPARTMENT OF ENVIRONMENTAL QUALITY'S PACKAGING WASTE REDUCTION BEST PRACTICES[4]

An Oregon manufacturer of bean dips and salsas packages product in 16-ounce polypropylene tubs. The tubs are frequently shipped twelve per carton. The conventional layout is "6 down, 2 up" (two layers of six tubs each). The resulting carton is very shallow and requires a total of 745 square inches of corrugated.

An alternative layout is "4 down, 3 up." In this approach, the carton holds three layers of four tubs each. The carton only requires 704 square inches of corrugated. It holds the same number of tubs but with a 5.6 percent reduction of fiber when compared to the conventional design. As an added advantage, the filled cartons ship more compactly on standard pallets, allowing 7.7 percent more product on a typical 40"×48" pallet.

The most efficient shape (least fiber per unit of volume) is a carton where the length and height (also referred to as "depth") are the same (or very similar), and the width is about half of the length.

A conventional layout (below) and more efficient layout that uses less material and allows more product per shipping pallet.

As the example at left illustrates, designers can also change the size of the case to match the size of the primary package better. It's easy to calculate the volume of a corrugated case by multiplying the height by width by depth. It's also easy to calculate the surface area of the corrugated board (height × width of each side, added together, including flaps). By rearranging the way products are stacked in a case, you may be able to maintain the required volume yet use less paper for the box. This could, in turn, save money in shipping.

PEELING AWAY THE LAYERS

One strategy for improving a packaging system's ecological profile is to design away some of the layers. This often means that your design performs multiple functions with a single layer so that additional layers become unnecessary.

For instance, let's say that you needed to get thousands of printed brochures to the homes or offices of customers. A typical solution would be to put the brochures in an envelope with a printed address and mail them. Yet it might cost less and use far less stuff if you planned ahead and designed the brochure as a self-mailer. Self-mailing is not uncommon (newsletters and catalogs are obvious examples). But many things that typically use envelopes could be reconceived as self-mailers. Over the years at Celery, we have created self-mailing letterhead, presentation folders, CD jewelcases, and portfolio booklets, to name a few. In each case, we tried to eliminate the material required for distribution (envelopes) by rethinking the design.

THE PRESIDIO
THOREAU CENTER FOR
SUSTAINABILITY

POST OFFICE BOX 29372
SAN FRANCISCO,
CALIFORNIA 94129-0372

415.561.3344 TELEPHONE
415.561.3345 FACSIMILE
TNS@NATURALSTEP.ORG

the NATURAL STEP

As part of an identity system overhaul for the environmental nonprofit group **The Natural Step**, Celery created a unique self-mailing letterhead. Each sheet has specially designed perforations and scores. The user simply prints the letter with an address on the back (which is easy with a duplex printer), folds on the score lines and seals the letter, adds a stamp, and mails—without using an envelope.

A very different strategy for designing away layers of packaging is to change the way that things get delivered. If you're asked to develop a brochure, for instance, you could post the brochure contents online and send a simple postcard driving traffic to the Web site. Or you could deliver the brochure by means other than the postal service.

Door-to-door delivery is usually the realm of pizza coupons and political flyers, but it has interesting potential for green designers. Because it is a manual process, the designer isn't limited to designs and materials that work with postal auto mation machinery. Perhaps the brochure hangs from a door knob. It could be held together with a tie string or a colorful rubber band, or placed in a reusable fabric bag. Any of these ideas could be more attention-grabbing and less wasteful than a standard envelope. If you are delivering to customers in a fairly small geographic area, it may actually be cheaper to hand-deliver than to pay for envelopes and postage.

Elephant Pharmacy is a retail chain based in Northern California that focuses on natural health and wellness products. Celery helped the company launch their first store with a unique direct mail campaign. Rather than starting from the "junk-mail" paradigm of a plastic bag door hanger stuffed with glossy coupons, we imagined the project as an opportunity to give a small gift to 30,000 people. This simple change of perspective impacted the whole project. The resulting "gift box" contained free samples of natural health and wellness products along with illustrated coupons. The mailer was constructed with recycled chip board and featured a pop-out door hanger, which made it completely recyclable. Each box was delivered with a fresh flower tucked into a paper belly-band. The flowers were the idea of Elephant's founder and CEO, who really embraced the concept of direct mail as a gift-giving opportunity. People hate junk mail, but they love flowers.

Two years later, Celery had the opportunity to help Elephant produce another direct mail campaign. By this time, the company had grown to four stores and their audience had expanded. We tried to replicate some of the unique user

The first generation promotion for **Elephant Pharmacy** (left) was a "gift box" delivered door-to-door with a fresh flower. The second generation promotion (right) was an interactive deck of cards held together by a rubber band.

experience from the gift box but substantially reduce the unit cost. The resulting design is a deck of cards held together by a rubber band. Each card has a bit of helpful advice on one side and a fun activity on the back. One card explains the benefits of yoga under the headline "Be flexible." The back of the card demonstrates "finger pilates" exercises that people can try, using the rubber band that held the cards together. Another card explains how to make a yin/yang flip card—again using the rubber band.

The idea here is to engage the reader and transform the packaging (a rubber band) into an essential part of the user experience. The piece was delivered as a door-hanger so we didn't need an outer envelope. The rubber band was made of natural latex,

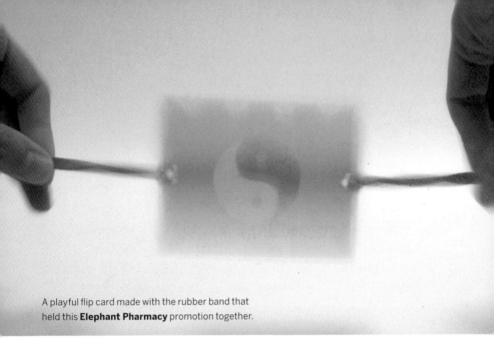

A playful flip card made with the rubber band that held this **Elephant Pharmacy** promotion together.

which is compostable, and the paper is 100 percent post-consumer recycled fiber. The cards were sized to make the most of the press sheet and were "chop cut" to minimize trim waste. All of this was invisible to the end user, but these efficiencies helped to make the piece a cost-effective manifestation of Elephant's brand.

Community supported agriculture (CSA) programs represent another interesting model for efficient distribution. Instead of going shopping for produce, people can subscribe directly to a nearby organic farm and receive whatever food is in season every week. This system provides consumers with fresh, seasonal, local produce and provides farmers with a steady source of income.

Let's look at how the CSA distribution system impacts packaging. Once a week, workers at Riverdog Farm in Northern California pack freshly harvested fruits and vegetables into corrugated shipping boxes. Lettuces and onions are loose in the box.

Asparagus spears are held together with a rubber band. Baby potatoes are held in a clear plastic bag. The boxes are loaded onto a truck and driven about ninety miles to a variety of drop-off spots in the San Francisco area. On my way home from work, I stop at one of these drop-off spots (a neighbor's front porch), sign my name on a list, and take a box of food home with me.

There are no bar codes, shrink wrap, or plastic clam-shell containers in this system. The produce does not move through multiple phases of distribution, warehousing, and shelf display. As a result, much of the packaging that we find in a typical supermarket is unnecessary. Furthermore, most of the packaging in a CSA system is reusable. When I pick up my veggie box each week, I return the box from the previous week. Finally, CSA programs can offer a superior user experience compared to shopping at the supermarket—I don't need to drive to the store or stand in line at the check-out counter.

What can graphic designers learn from community supported agriculture? In addition to designing greener packages, can we imagine modes of distribution that allow products to be delivered without extraneous disposable packaging? Most importantly, can an eco-designed packaging solution enable a superior user experience? SEE PAGE 176

Slow down (you move too fast). It contradicts our deeply ingrained notions of efficiency, but moving stuff rapidly around the world is not very efficient. Or rather, it is time-efficient, but that comes at the expense of ecological and economic efficiency. Generally speaking, the faster you ship something, the more greenhouse gases you cause to be emitted. E-mail is a notable exception to that rule: Messages are delivered nearly instantaneously, anywhere in the world, with a relatively tiny ecological footprint. Other than that, your best bet is ocean freight, rail, or truck (in that order). Air freight emits a mind-blowing thirty-three times more greenhouse gases than shipping by boat! That simple statement, *"I'll overnight it to you"* suddenly seems less "efficient."

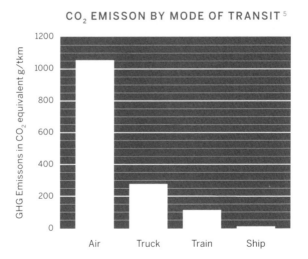

CO$_2$ EMISSON BY MODE OF TRANSIT [5]

If a project is going to travel long distances, graphic designers can help reduce climate impacts by building enough time into schedules to allow for slower-mode transport. It turns out that procrastination is the enemy of green design. If schedules are too tight for slow-mode transport, perhaps the project would be a good candidate for electronic delivery.

Digitize, Decentralize, On Demand. One interesting concept that graphic designers should consider when working on high-volume global projects is distributed printing. Rather than producing thousands or millions of one thing in one place and shipping them around the world (a print-then-distribute model), it often makes more sense to ship digital files to printers in several regions and print only the amounts that are required for that region (a distribute-then-print model).

This scenario is made even more appealing when it's combined with on-demand printing, which can reduce excess printing and warehouse obsolescence. The result can be a significant savings of time and money and a drastically lower environmental impact.

Hybrid publishing. Delivering information on the Web is often cheaper than printed communication and, in most situations, causes less ecological harm. However, printed media have some great advantages in terms of user experience. Print is tactile, stable, and persistent, so audiences often perceive the printed word to be more authoritative and reliable than digital media. Print is portable and autonomous (you don't need to power down a brochure for take-off). Also, print works well as a "push" medium, meaning that audiences can receive designed messages without making any special effort (such as typing in a particular Web address).

One challenge for green designers is to find ways to use low-impact digital media without sacrificing an effective user experience. This often results in a "hybrid" publishing model that combines print and digital media into an integrated campaign.

It's easy to see the development of this hybrid model in the progression of Hewlett-Packard's Global Citizenship Report.

In 2002, Celery designed HP's first such report, which was then called the **Social and Environmental Responsibility Report**. This was a conventional, sixty-eight page printed report.

003 Global Citizenship Report

In 2003, the name changed to
the **Global Citizenship Report**.
This time it was a seventy-six
page report, printed on 100 percent post-consumer paper on an
HP Indigo digital press—a first for
HP. We also created a PDF file of
the report, which was downloadable from HP 's Web site.

2004 Abridged Global Citizenship Report
See more details in the full report at http://www.hp.com/go/

2004 Global Citizenship Report

In 2004, we printed a twenty
page abridged report in addition
to the eighty page full report and
also created a downloadable PDF
of the full report.

In 2006, we switched to an HTML-based Web site and a downloadable PDF for the full report, but we did not print the full report. The only printed communication was a twenty page abridged report.

The evolution of this project demonstrates a steady shift from a singular physical object toward a family of materials in several media, targeted at several different audiences. The project arguably has a smaller environmental footprint now than it did in 2002, but it's also far more likely to reach its target audience.

Our systems for distribution and packaging greatly influence the form and the ecological impact of the work that graphic designers do. These systems are too important and too ripe for innovation for green designers to ignore. Before accepting the existing system, designers can ask questions like: *What is the ideal way of distributing this content?*; *What materials would support the ephemeral or durable nature of my packaging?*; or *Should this design be delivered as a single piece in a single medium, or multiple targeted pieces in multiple media?* The answers to these questions may inspire fresh creativity and better design solutions.

In 2007, the full report was web-only. Instead of creating a down-loadable PDF, we created a "Custom Report" tool that allowed users to assemble sections of the report for easy printing at home. In shifting from print and PDF to HTML, we restructured the contents of the report to work better in a nonlinear medium. Instead of an "abridged report" that attempts to convey "a little bit about everything," we created a twenty page Customer Report that was more narrowly targeted for major HP customers. This piece was translated and localized into nineteen regional versions, which were printed locally. We also created a global CD-ROM that contained all 19 versions of the Customer Report along with other multimedia content. SEE PAGE 179 FOR MORE INFORMATION.

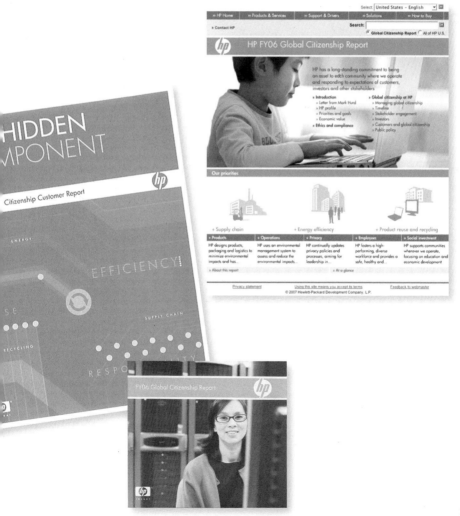

GOOD IMPRESSIONS

DESIGN FOR MANUFACTURING

I got a big lesson in the importance of design for manufacturing from a print job that went wrong. The project was the *Green Building Guidelines,* produced by the county of Alameda, California, for homeowners and building contractors. Alameda was one of the first municipalities in the United States to actively and aggressively promote the benefits of green building, and this project was their primary means of communicating on the subject. I thought this would be a great case study for green graphics: The design was

attractive, the content was interesting, the paper was 100 percent recycled, and it had the potential to make a positive difference in the world.

At the press check for the cover of the *Guidelines,* I was presented with a large printed press sheet that was mostly blank. More that half the surface area on many thousands of press sheets was wasted—destined for the recycle bin before it even left the factory floor. This great green project had somehow turned out to be an efficiency disaster and a big waste of money.

Toward the end of the project, our client had asked for a simple pocket on the back cover to hold a list of local green businesses. We added a standard 4-inch pocket and didn't think much more about it. However, that simple little pocket meant the printer could only fit 2-up, rather than the typical 4-up, on a 26"×40" press sheet, and the rest of the press sheet went to waste. And since we were already on press when I discovered this, it was too late to change much of anything.

Our investigation uncovered a long list of things that could have been done differently, but two things stuck out: We could have communicated better with the printer, and we could have thought about how our design would be produced. **By the time a design gets into manufacturing, it is usually too late to make the production process more efficient**. The designer needs to learn about manufacturing processes and plan ahead.

The conventional pocket design requires twice as much paper compared with the **corner pocket**.

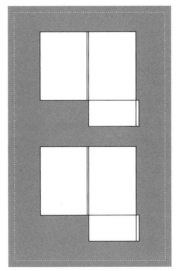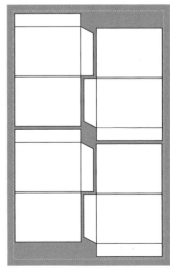

Fortunately, the *Green Building Guidelines* were a great success. Alameda County did several reprints and the State of California eventually adopted the *Guidelines* as a state-wide standard. The reprints gave us an opportunity to learn from our mistakes and come up with a better solution. We laid out the full press sheet and tried to create an effective pocket from the available space. The result was an L-shaped "corner pocket" made up of a two inch flap across the bottom and a two inch flap on the side edge. The pocket held papers more securely than a conventional pocket, cost the same to assemble, and enabled the printer to get four covers on a single press sheet. Win, win, win.

Designing a press sheet, it turns out, is an easy way for graphic designers to get the most out of a print run. It allows us to see problems and apply creative thinking before it's too late. It also forces designers to understand the manufacturing process, which is essential if you hope to make that process more efficient. SEE PAGE 114.

A PRESS FOR EVERY PROJECT: SMALL, MEDIUM, LARGE

The "design backwards" process for print manufacturing goes something like this: The quantity of the print run → determines type of printing press → determines paper options available and press sheet size → which drives the structure of a designed layout. In other words, we need to understand the full sweep of the printing process before we decide on the size and structure of our designs. Printing 4 million units of something is a very different process from printing 4,000 units, which is different from printing 40 units. Those differences should be reflected in the design strategy.

Setting up a conventional printing press is slow and expensive. In four-color process printing, four plates are output and mounted onto rollers, ink wells are filled, and paper is fed through the press as ink levels and roller pressure is adjusted. All of the prints made during this make-ready phase are waste, and it's often a significant amount of waste. Most printers assume 10 percent of the paper used on any job will go to make-ready waste. That can add up to a lot of paper in the waste heap.

One way to measure the eco-efficiency of printing is to compare the amount of waste created with the amount of usable printed material. Conventional offset printing starts with a fairly large deficit in this measure because of its long set-up process. The set-up time required will vary depending on each printer's equipment and experience, but it generally makes sense to run small jobs on small presses. Some printers say that a standard 40″ press is not eco-efficient for runs of less than 5,000 impressions. Others say the press should run continually for an hour or more after set-up in order to consider a job eco-efficient. It is not always possible to achieve optimal efficiency, but the designer should be conscious of how their work is going to be produced and communicate with the printer in order to avoid unnecessary waste.

A recent comprehensive life cycle assessment performed in Denmark found that the printing process is the largest contributor to the environmental impact of most printed materials—more than the combined impacts of paper and ink. SEE GRAPH AT RIGHT. The environmental impact of printing is determined during three key phases: set-up, run-time, and clean-up. Each phase presents distinct environmental challenges.

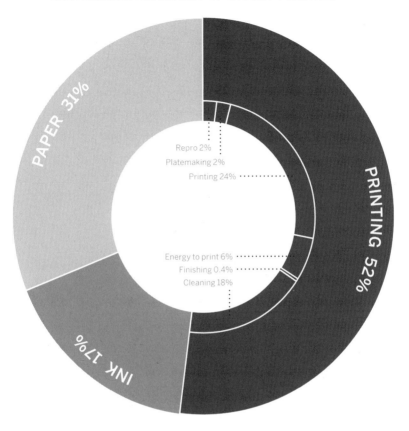

PAPER 31%

PRINTING 52%

INK 17%

Repro 2%
Platemaking 2%
Printing 24%

Energy to print 6%
Finishing 0.4%
Cleaning 18%

SET-UP Large amounts of paper waste and ink waste are produced during the "make-ready" process.

RUN-TIME Fountain solutions based on alcohol or alcohol substitutes are required for conventional offset lithography. These are a major source of air pollution in the form of volatile organic compounds (VOCs). Also, printing presses consume lots of energy. This energy is typically generated from fossil fuels, resulting in significant greenhouse gas emissions.

CLEAN-UP Toxic solvents (another major source of VOCs) are often used to clean the rollers and ink wells of conventional offset printing presses.

That's a pretty wide array of environmental issues: paper waste, toxic materials, energy impacts, and air pollution. There are also other impacts, such as toxic chemicals used for photographic printing plates and impacts associated with petroleum-based inks, which contribute a smaller proportion of the total impact of offset printing.

Because of this complexity, it's often difficult to compare the relative benefits of various printing options. Competing technologies may improve particular environmental attributes under particular circumstances, but no single solution resolves every aspect of the problem. However, it is possible to identify preferred technologies for small, medium, and large print runs.

SMALL. For "short run" print jobs (1–1000 impressions), digital printing is a clear environmental leader. Digital presses such as Hewlett Packard's Indigo or Kodak's NexPress virtually eliminate make-ready paper waste, ink waste, and clean-up solvents.

Digital printing benefits: Low paper waste for make-readies; low ink waste; and no clean-up solvents.

Digital printing limitations: Digital presses require specific surface qualities so paper options can be limited. This makes it a bit harder to specify post-consumer recycled papers and papers with unique colors and textures. It's not impossible, but sales reps and press operators are often not accustomed to working with materials beyond the standard fare.

Because they don't require a make-ready process, digital presses emit fewer VOCs than conventional offset litho presses on short print runs. However, as the length of the run increases, this particular environmental advantage becomes less pronounced.[7] For this and other reasons, digital presses are usually best suited to shorter runs.

MEDIUM. On medium-length print runs (roughly 1,000–50,000), sheetfed offset lithography typically offers the best combination of price, quality, flexibility, and environmental impact. Legal regulations for allowable VOC emissions vary widely by region. In areas with tight regulations, most printers have switched to low VOC press formulations. In other regions printers remain a major source of air pollution. Graphic designers should know about two major technologies that can improve the environmental impact of offset lithography: waterless printing and UV printing.

Waterless printing is an integrated press and ink technology that eliminates most of the VOC emissions related to offset lithography. The process uses silicone-coated blankets on the press rollers, which repel ink from areas that are not intended to print. This differs from the conventional printing process where "ink resist" is accomplished with the help of fountain solutions, frequently made of water. Traditionally, the water is mixed with high-VOC alcohol, which speeds up evaporation. By eliminating the water, you eliminate the need for rapid evaporation, and hence the need for VOCs. Waterless printing systems are typically used on "heat set" presses that use special ovens to help dry the inks.

"The main sources of VOCs are the damping system and cleaning solvents. In fact, eliminating the damping solution by, for example, switching to waterless printing may reduce VOC emissions by 50 percent or more."

—Sandra Rothenberg, *Environmental Management in Lithographic Printing*

Another large portion of the VOC pollution emitted in printing comes from the solvent-based solutions used to wash printing presses. Some printers are now using "water-washable" inks, which eliminate the need for solvent-based cleaning agents. Presses can be cleaned with simple soap and water. This combination of waterless printing and water-washable inks can virtually eliminate VOCs from the pressroom floor.

UV printing is another integrated press and ink technology which eliminates most of the VOCs from the offset printing process. UV inks are made up of pigments suspended in a liquid medium that hardens when exposed to ultraviolet light. UV presses have large ultraviolet lamps next to each roller which set the inks as the paper passes through. This eliminates the need for VOC-emitting fountain solutions on press. Since UV inks don't dry on the rollers or in ink wells, they can often be cleaned up without solvent-based washes. Also, since the inks set instantaneously, UV presses are often able to run faster than conventional offset presses, which helps reduce energy usage.

Waterless and UV printing both involve major investments in new equipment and training for conventional printers. As a result, they may not be available in every market, or they might be prohibitively expensive for certain projects.

Graphic designers can also request that printers use VOC–free ink sets. This is a new generation of press formulations, increasingly popular in regions with tight air regulations, which do not require any special equipment.

LARGE. Very large print projects (50,000 or more impressions) typically run on web offset or roto-gravure presses. These presses use huge rolls of paper rather than sheets, and they run at high speeds. Most of these presses are heatset, which means the printed paper passes through ovens in order to speed up drying time. Some web printers are installing UV systems on their web presses in lieu of traditional heatset ovens. This eliminates most of the VOC emissions from the process and reduces energy consumption.

Several large web and gravure printers, such as Quad/Graphics, operate sealed presses with VOC capture and combustion systems. The captured VOC gases are burned and the resulting heat is fed back into the heatset ovens. This cuts energy use and prevents VOC emissions to the outside air.

The Rochester Institute of Technology Printing Industry Center has published several helpful research reports on this topic.[8]

Renewable energy is another way to improve the environmental impact of printing. Printing presses are a major consumer of electricity. To reduce the greenhouse gas pollution associated with generating that electricity, a handful of progressive printers are now buying renewable energy credits—in some cases offsetting all of the energy they consume. This enables printers to claim that their operations are "climate neutral" even though they are still using energy and creating greenhouse gases.

THINK INK

Printing ink is made up of two main components: the medium and the pigment. The medium keeps pigment particles suspended while the ink is on press. Once ink transfers to a piece of paper, the liquid medium must quickly set (dry out) so that the pigment forms a stable bond. One way to make this happen is to make the medium extremely "volatile" so it evaporates when exposed to air. Unfortunately, the resulting volatile organic compounds (VOCs) cause air pollution and are bad for press workers' health.

It is best to **ask specifically for low-VOC inks**. Standard inks may be formulated with up to 35 percent VOC content, but low-VOC formulations are available from several ink companies. Liberty Ink is a line of zero-VOC inks marketed by Kohl & Madden for conventional sheetfed offset presses. Another option, of course, is to print with UV inks, which don't rely on evaporation to set the inks. SEE PAGE 110.

Designers can also **specify vegetable-based inks** instead of petroleum inks. Vegetable inks (based on sunflower oil, soy oil, canola oil, …) typically have lower VOC levels than petroleum inks, which is good.

Be aware, however, that ink labels are not always what they seem. The "Soy Ink" label, which was promoted for years by the American Soybean Association, means that an ink contains a designated minimum percentage of soybean oil (as little as 7 percent for some instances). So an ink could be more than 90 percent petroleum oil and still qualify for the "soy ink" label. The label also suggests lower VOC levels than conventional ink, but it makes no specific claim. If you are interested in avoiding air pollution and petroleum inks, it helps to ask a prospective printer for the actual percentage of vegetable oil and VOC content in the inks they use.

AVOIDING TOXIC METALS

The color choices that designers make can affect the environmental impact of printed materials once they end up in a landfill, in an incinerator, or at a de-inking facility. That's because some inks get their vibrant color from metals in the pigments. The most toxic "CAMALS" substances (cadmium, arsenic, mercury, antimony, lead, selenium) have been phased out of conventional printing inks in North America. As far as we know, the remaining metals are not harmful to people in the concentrations normally used on printed materials. However, those metals can concentrate in the ash from incinerators or sludge from de-inking facilities (creating hazardous waste issues) and can potentially leach from landfills into water supplies.

Metallic and fluorescent spot colors have the highest proportions of metals. They usually contain high levels of **copper** and **zinc**. Spot colors that are formulated with the Pantone® Warm Red mixing base contain **barium** from a pigment called Red Lake C. Certain blue and green colors contain **copper**. The U.S. EPA's "Section 313" list provides a resource listing which colors in the Pantone Matching System® contain notably high levels of metals. It is usually easy to find suitable replacements that do not rely on worrisome metal pigments. SEE PAGE 188. In 2007, Pantone released the Goe™ color system, which does not use Red Lake c for the Warm Red mixing base (relying instead on the pigment Yellow Shade Napthol). This makes the search for nontoxic spot color inks easier.

Another metal of concern is **cobalt**. This is used in many inks as a drying agent. Several ink manufacturers, including Sun Chemical, now offer inks without cobalt driers.

FINISHING AND BINDING

The last phases of the print manufacturing process are finishing and bindery. As with every other step on the "design backwards" journey, these areas are ripe for eco-innovation.

Trim and Die Cutting

In offset printing, designs are typically run with multiple impressions on a press sheet. After printing, the press sheet is folded and cut into individual sheets. Since designers are often unaware of the details of print production, it is easy to end up with a design that fits poorly on a press sheet and leaves a great deal of trim waste. As we discussed previously, designers can avoid that waste by "designing" the press sheet.

The first step in designing a press sheet is to find out what size press sheet you will be printing on. That is influenced by several variables: the paper you choose (specifically, what sizes are available from the mill), how many total impressions you are printing, and the size of the press that your printer has. It is inefficient to do short runs on large presses so it is important to match the right size press with your print run. SEE PAGE 108. If you ask, your printer should be able to tell you early on what sheet size they expect to use.

The next step is to calculate how many impressions will fit on each press sheet. Start with the sheet size and subtract a half inch margin on all sides for the color density bars and gripper (where the press grabs the paper). What's left is your maximum live area on the sheet. If you start with a 26" × 40" sheet, for instance, then subtract the margins, you end up with a live area of 25" × 39". Divide the width and height of the live area into a grid, and then experiment with formats and sizes that work for the design and also fit efficiently on the press sheet. Be sure to leave ¼" of space for the trim marks around the individual impressions.

25" divides well to ...	39" divides well to ...
2 × 12" + trim	2 × 19" + trim
3 × 8" + trim	3 × 13"
4 × 6" + trim	4 × 9.5" + trim
5 × 5"	5 × 7.75" + trim

With a little forethought, the designer can consider several potential formats (for instance, printing 4-up, 6-up, or 8-up) prior to settling on a final design. If none of the efficient formats will work for your design, it may be possible to request a different sheet size. As you engage with the printer in a dialogue about press sheet layout, you'll also learn a great deal about grain direction, ink balance, and other printing issues.

The dimensions calculated above are prior to trimming. If imagery or zones of color "bleed" off the edge of a page, then that page gets trimmed twice on each edge—once to "chop" apart the pages on the press sheet and a second time to trim off the edges of the individual page. Multipage booklets are usually trimmed a third time after bindery to clean up the outside edges. Each trim generates cut-off waste. Designers can eliminate at least one of the trims (and the associated waste) by avoiding "bleeds" or finding other ways to allow simple "chop cuts." This won't necessarily mean that you use fewer press sheets, but it does shift material from waste into usable design space. The result is that the designer has more real estate to work with, without using extra paper.

Die cutting is different from trimming because the cutting is done with a shaped metal blade mounted to a backer board, rather than straight blade. The good thing about die cutting is that it is often possible to "nest" multiple impressions so that flaps are not surrounded by wasted space. This is especially useful for folders and packaging projects, which often require odd-shaped patterns. SEE PAGES 104, 177.

However, keep in mind that die cutting also generates trim waste. Tabbed divider pages are a good example of this. In order to get a tab that protrudes ½" past the edge of the trim size of a booklet, it is usually necessary to start with a sheet that is 1½" inches wider than the rest of the booklet. Nearly all of that extra width is trim waste just to leave a small tab sticking out.

Celery took a different approach on a workbook we designed for the Alameda County green building program. Rather than creating standard protruding tabs on chapter dividers, we created a simple "fold-out" tab. The divider pages have a c-shaped cut near the right side of the page. This creates a flap, which the end user can fold over to make a protruding tab. A straight vertical slot keeps the tab in place. This type of internal die

Tabbed dividers for the **Alameda County Green Building Workbook** are specially designed to eliminate trim waste.

cutting does not generate any extra waste and enables us to provide tabs without starting from an over-sized sheet of paper. Similar to the "corner pocket" (DISCUSSED ON PAGE 104), this is an example of how the quest to eliminate trim waste can lead to new design approaches and new user experiences.

This simple process of formatting a press sheet can have a profound impact on how designers practice their craft. It forces the designer to think about how things will be produced, it increases communication between designer and printer, and it can prevent costly and wasteful designs from making it into production. In many cases, the designer can trim a fraction of an inch from the size of a piece and drastically increase the efficiency of the print run. Initially, you may need to ask lots of questions. Eventually, it becomes part of your knowledge base, and you are able to push beyond standard processes.

Mechanical Bindery

Mechanical binding is generally the most recyclable type of bindery. Saddle stitching with staples is the most common mechanical binding. Wire-o and side-stapling are also popular for certain industries. Metal staples and wire coils separate easily from the paper fiber in the repulping process and are removed with magnets from the slurry. The Spiral Binding Company in New Jersey makes all their base wire from recycled steel; thus, a wire-o binding can be both recyclable and previously recycled.

Ring binders and other loose-leaf binding systems offer the added benefit of being re-usable. Vancouver Bookbinding makes customized binders that can be made with post-consumer recycled paperboard. The Sustainable Group sells a line of pre-fab binders from recycled board, which can be silk screened or stickered with custom designs.

The Thinkbook journal uses a mechanical binding that's something of a hybrid. SEE PAGE 56. Individual signatures are saddle stitched with raised "loop" staples, creating a series of twenty-page booklets. Those booklets are then bound together with a flexible rubber strap that attaches to the cover material. The result is a reusable system that lays flat and doesn't require bulky, heavy metal rings. Smythe sewing and "Singer" stitching are also mechanical bindings, typically used on high-end pieces. When these are recycled, the thread used in smythe sewing becomes part of the pulp fiber. Comb binding is a mechanical binding, but the combs are typically made from PVC plastic, which should be avoided.

Adhesive Bindery

Adhesive bindings hold pages together by applying glue to the spine edge. Three main types of adhesives are used for this purpose, and they each have different environmental profiles.

PVA (polyvinyl acetate) is a water-based synthetic "white" glue, similar to Elmer's glue and common carpenter's wood glue. For binding paper, it is applied at room temperature, and it sets into a flexible emulsion. PVA is not as strong as some competing adhesives, and it sets more slowly. It's also made from nonrenewable petroleum. However, it is nontoxic, is commonly available, and is compatible with established recycling systems.

EcoSynthetix in Michigan has introduced a new adhesive that shares many of the advantages of PVA, yet comes from a renewable resource. It is made from corn starch that has been milled to a nanoparticle size. McDonald's fast food chain has used this adhesive on clam-shell hamburger packaging. Wisdom Adhesives makes a protein-based bookbinding adhesive called GreenBond.

PUR (polyurethane) hotmelt adhesives are often considered a premium binding material, but they've grown in popularity over the past decade because they can be used sparingly and they create incredibly strong bonds. PURs form a chemical matrix when they are exposed to moisture in the atmosphere. They don't release VOCs or hazardous air pollutants (HAPs). While they are not water soluble, PURs are stable once they have set. That means the adhesive doesn't mix with pulp fibers during recycling, so it can usually be filtered out. The hardened PUR ends up as part of the de-inking sludge.

EVA (ethylene vinyl acetate) hotmelt adhesive is the type used in "hot glue guns" and also in many book binderies. EVA is relatively inexpensive, easy to apply, low VOC, and low toxicity. However, this type of adhesive softens when reheated, which can cause problems in some recycling processes.

Several teams of researchers around the world are researching super-strong adhesives that mimic the mechanical properties of geckos, mussels, and other animals. These biomimetic adhesives may soon enable us to instantaneously bind surfaces together without any toxic solvents or permanent resins.

DESIGN FOR SMART PRINTING

In recent years, print vendors have increasingly begun touting their green credentials to the design community. It certainly would be nice if designers could simply specify "green printing" and feel confident that everything would be taken care of. Unfortunately, that is not the case. In order to significantly change the status quo, we need to change the way we design, not just the vendors we use. While it is encouraging that printers recognize the importance of environmental impacts, the chorus of competing claims can also lead to confusion. The only way for designers to sort through the marketing noise is to understand what actually happens in the pressroom and bindery. Rather than marketing pitches, green designers really need relationships with printers who share their values and are willing to identify and avoid unnecessary manufacturing waste before ink reaches paper.

THE NATURE
OF PAPER

Paper is the central stuff of graphic design. We use it for nearly everything we do, and we use a lot of it. The good news, from an environmental perspective, is that paper **can** be an ecologically intelligent medium for our messages. It is made from a renewable resource, and it is compatible with many durable uses like books as well as ephemeral uses like secondary packaging. Also, the fibers in paper can continue to hold some material value after their initial use through recycling or can return to nature through composting.

The bad news is that our collective appetite for paper is seemingly insatiable and the methods by which we typically harvest fiber and make paper are incredibly damaging to the environment. We have stripped much of the world's old forests bare in an attempt to feed this appetite for paper. A 1997 World Resources Institute (WRI) report[9] estimated that "seventy-six countries have already lost all of their original forest cover and a further eleven countries have less than five percent left."

In their "Paper Cuts" report [10], the Worldwatch Institute wrote:

> Global paper and paperboard consumption has been increasing so rapidly that it has overwhelmed gains made by recycling. So while the amount of material recovered has increased sevenfold since 1961 and the share of recycled content paper in the fiber supply has nearly doubled, the total volume of virgin wood pulp and paper consumed and waste generated continues to rise, overtaking these important successes.

In addition to driving forest destruction, paper production consumes an enormous amount of energy and therefore has a very large greenhouse gas impact. Taken together, the facts show that the paper industry is the fourth largest industrial producer of carbon dioxide, accounting for 9 percent of our greenhouse gas emissions. This is far from sustainable, and graphic designers are in a unique position to effect positive change.

EVERY DAY ARBOR DAY

After a couple of years of running Celery, we had collected a hefty binder full of paper resources. Every time we found a reference to environmentally preferable papers, we requested samples and information. When we needed to specify a paper, we would run to the binder and try to find the best match. We eventually decided to pull together a resource of the best-in-class papers available on the market. The initial goal was to get our clients involved in the paper selection process. As the project took shape, though, it also became an opportunity to promote the greenest of the green papers to a wider audience of graphic designers.

We have updated the **Ecological Guide to Paper** several times (see below). The Guide taught us that you don't need to wait for a client in order to put an interesting project together. If the idea is solid, collaborators will often pitch in to make it happen. It also taught us that education is a powerful tool for design. Most of the materials we receive in the mail are just trying to sell us something. When something useful comes, audiences tend to take notice.

The result was Celery's Ecological Guide to Paper. On one side, it was a poster with the headline, "Every Day Arbor Day." The other side had information about the top 50 environmentally preferable papers. Celery did the research and designed the poster. The San Francisco Chapter of AIGA agreed to help us get printing and paper donations, and they distributed the Guide to all Bay Area AIGA members. We also got a small grant from the County of Alameda, and some writing help from a nonprofit called Fiber Futures. SEE PAGE 192.

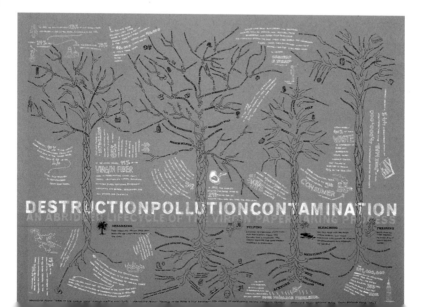

FIBER + WATER + ENERGY = PAPER

The paper we use for printed communications is typically made up of wood fiber plus a variety of surface treatments, such as starch, latex, and clay, and dyes that determine color and brightness. Paper also carries a significant "ecological shadow" of energy consumption, bleaching chemicals, and water used in its production.

In 2005, Fox River Paper Company asked Celery to help them promote their recycled paper lines. We noted that the field was already cluttered with paper companies touting their eco-friendliness, making it difficult to gain traction by producing more of the same.

Building upon our experience with the Ecological Guide to Paper, we decided to use this as an opportunity for us to learn—and then teach the broader design community—about best practices relating to paper and the environment. This educational approach helps establish authenticity, which makes the audience more receptive to learning about Fox River Paper's products.

Working with the writer Colin Berry, we then crafted "calls to action" relating to fiber, water, and energy issues. This became the framework for **Fox River Paper's Nature of Paper** brochure and a series of newsletters.

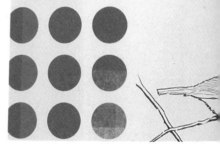

FIBER. WATER. ENERGY.

These are the most fundamental elements of the paper-making process. They are also the key factors that determine paper's overall environmental impact. At Fox River Paper Co., we focus on each of these areas in order to offer our customers a comprehensive ecological solution: the highest quality uncoated paper made in a responsible manner with materials and energy sources that minimize environmental impacts.

As you choose paper for your corporate communications, you can take several key actions to minimize the environmental impacts of the paper you use:

Designers who try to understand the ecological impact of the paper they use must confront a flurry of competing logos and marketing claims from paper companies. Each company promotes a range of single-attribute advantages for their products, making it difficult to compare competing products. If we understand the multiple environmental issues facing the industry, then it's easier to separate substance from fluff. We can divide those issues into three basic categories: **fiber issues**, **water issues**, and **energy issues**.

Maximize post-consumer recycled fiber.

Post-consumer fiber comes mainly from municipal and office recycling programs—not directly from forests. By using paper with a high percentage of post-consumer fiber, you can reduce the demand for virgin pulp and thus reduce pressure on forest ecosystems.

Fox River Paper Co. is an industry leader in manufacturing recycled papers. Since the early 1980's, we have continually increased the level of post-consumer waste in our papers. We currently make more than 200 different colors and finish combinations containing post-consumer fiber, representing nearly 70% of our offerings. These sheets range from 30% to 100% post-consumer recycled content.

WATER ENERGY PAPER

FIBER ISSUES

It's a long way from the design studio to the remote forest eco-system, but the paper choices designers make directly impact what happens in large swaths of the world's forestland. We may think that we are in the business of fonts and images, but our fiber consumption also makes graphic designers major players in the forest products industry. As such, our choices impact deforestation, species extinction, global warming, and other global environmental issues.

Designers can do three things to minimize the negative impacts of the fiber we use:

- Use post-consumer recycled fiber,

- Use sustainably harvested virgin fiber, and

- Use tree-free alternative fibers.

Post-consumer recycled (PCR) fiber comes from collection programs, not from the forest. When we use it, we are not putting pressure on forest ecosystems. We are also supporting paper collection programs by providing a market for collected fiber. Both of these are ecological positives. High-quality papers with up to 100 percent post-consumer recycled fiber are readily available for uncoated offset printing. Because of increased public demand over the past two decades, high-percentage PCR paper is increasingly available for coated sheets and web presses. A growing number of magazines and catalog retailers are using these sheets.

FSC

Sustainably harvested fiber is virgin fiber that is produced through responsible forest management. "Responsible" is a vague and slippery term, so it is important to demand third-party certification. The Forest Stewardship Council has emerged as the premier standard for assessing the sustainability of forest management practices. In order to use the FSC certification logo on their products, a forest products company must submit their activities for review by auditors. Another well-respected certification is the Ancient Forest Friendly program sponsored by the Markets Initiative group.

The FSC forestry guidelines are built around ten sets of principles that deal with various aspects of forest management and ecosystem health:

1. Compliance with laws and FSC principles

2. Clearly defined use rights and responsibilities

3. Recognition and respect of indigenous peoples' rights

4. Long-term social and economic well-being of forest workers and local communities

5. Ensuring a wide range of benefits from the forest

6. Conservation of biological diversity, water resources, soils, and fragile ecosystems, thereby maintaining the integrity of the forest

7. Long-term, written management plan

8. Ongoing monitoring and assessment

9. Maintenance of high conservation value forests

10. Additional restrictions regarding plantations

The North American paper industry is gradually moving from a model of resource extraction (similar to the mining and oil industries) to a continuously regenerating agricultural model not dependent on disturbing pristine ecosystems. However, the paper industry is still responsible for 40 percent of all industrial deforestation worldwide. Graphic designers can help accelerate the transition to sustainable forestry and protect the rare remaining ancient forests by demanding FSC certification or Ancient Forest Friendly certification of all the virgin fiber paper they use.

The next step for the paper industry is to go beyond conventional industrial agriculture to something akin to organic agriculture. FSC-certified forestry is far better than clear-cuts of ancient forest, but the standard still allows the maintenance of large-scale tree farms that support very little biodiversity. Also, certifications are typically set up as "minimal" standards. They help establish certain practices in the mainstream, but they don't necessarily drive innovation. The real market leaders are often performing well beyond the minimal standard and those are the companies we should try to support.

Alternative fibers are another way to avoid damaging forests through your paper purchases because they come from a fiber source other than trees. Trees are not an ideal source of fiber for paper: They take a long time to grow and are not particularly space efficient. Wood was a cheap and plentiful resource when the Western paper industry developed, and the technologies and infrastructure of the industry are built around turning trees into paper. That means that alternative fibers must compete with a well-entrenched incumbent.

Bamboo is the alternative fiber that has gained the most traction in the North American paper market. It grows faster than wood, and it can be regrown from established roots without replanting. That helps to minimize topsoil loss. However, most bamboo comes from Asia and must be transported long distances—which requires significant amounts of energy.

Kenaf, hemp, and flax are fast-growing crops that have been used for papermaking. Several kenaf and hemp products have made it to market, but none has been a big success so far. These and other dedicated crops hold the promise of shifting our fiber source to annually renewable crops that can grow with few pesticides in many climates.

Agricultural residue, or agri-pulp, is perhaps the most promising fiber source because it makes use of the parts of an agricultural crop that are not used for food or another primary purpose. In this way, agri-pulp makes the most of a waste material and doesn't require dedicated agricultural land. Sugar cane bagasse has made some inroads in the North American paper market. Several manufacturers incorporate bagasse into uncoated papers that are available to designers. Wheat straw, banana fiber, and rice straw are all being used in other parts of the world. So far, though, no major North American paper manufacturer has made a big commitment to these promising fiber sources.

Cotton linters have been used for many years in high-end papers. Linters are the relatively short fibers left over after a cotton plant has been harvested and processed for textiles. Most paper marketed as "cotton" in North America is made with linters. Manufacturers can classify this fiber as "recycled" because it makes use of agricultural waste. It's worth noting, however, that conventional cotton agriculture consumes enormous quantities of toxic pesticides and fertilizers. A few small paper companies have chosen to support organic growers and steer clear of highly polluting conventional cotton.

One final "fiber" source to consider is no fiber at all. Synthetic papers have been in development for specialty markets for well over a decade, and a few producers are offering these for offset and web printing in North America. William McDonough's book *Cradle to Cradle* was printed on a synthetic paper in order to make a point—that we should not limit ourselves to the dominant palette of materials if we can imagine a better system. In theory, if there were a return and recycling infrastructure for this type of material, it could be remade and recirculated indefinitely. In practice, we're not anywhere near that situation, but it definitely raises a good challenge for designers.

WATER ISSUES

The huge paper making machines that create the paper we use start with a slurry mix of roughly 98 percent water. It is no surprise, then, that most mills are located on the banks of large rivers. The paper and pulp mills impact river ecosystems because of the **quantity** of water they use and because of the water **quality** of their effluent.

Designers can do three things to minimize the negative water impacts from the paper they use:

- Use Process Chlorine Free and Totally Chlorine Free fiber,

- Support closed-loop pulp and paper mills, and

- Use post-consumer recycled fiber (it requires a lot less water).

The paper industry's water **quality** problems stem largely from chlorine-based chemicals used to bleach paper pulp. When chlorine combines with wood and water, it produces trace amounts of dioxin, a chemical that is extremely toxic, persists in the environment, and bioaccumulates, meaning it stays in the food chain as contaminated plants and animals are eaten by other animals. Since pulp mills use large quantities of river water and release effluent containing chlorine back into the rivers, they have had a devastating and long-lasting impact on the health of river ecosystems. This has left us all with a legacy of dioxin in our body fat and breast milk, which will persist for many generations to come.

Because of increased regulation and public pressure, the North American paper industry has largely eliminated chlorine gas in pulp mills. For the most part, North American pulp mills shifted to bleaching with chlorine derivatives like chlorine dioxide, which reduce chlorine emissions by 90 percent or more. The paper that results from this pulp is commonly labeled Elemental Chlorine Free (ECF). European pulp mills, meanwhile, shifted primarily to more advanced systems based on oxygen or ozone, which eliminate chlorine altogether. The paper made with this bleaching technology is labeled Totally Chlorine Free (TCF) when applied to virgin fiber and Process Chlorine Free (PCF) when applied to recycled fiber. ECF pulping is certainly better than chlorine-bleached pulp, which is still produced in large quantities in many developing countries, but TCF/PCF pulp is better.

In addition to the quality of water emissions, there are serious environmental impacts related to the **quantity** of water the paper industry uses. The pulp and paper industry is the number one industrial user of water worldwide. Fresh water supply is rapidly becoming a worldwide environmental crisis on a similar scale to global warming. The paper industry is going to need to reduce its reliance on this precious resource, and graphic designers can help to speed the transition.

Innovative paper producers are moving toward "closed-loop" or Totally Effluent Free (TEF) manufacturing. Filtration technologies now exist that allow pulp and paper mills to continually reuse water. As a result, TEF mills can drastically reduce the amount of fresh water they draw from rivers and wells, and the amount of wastewater they release into the environment. The water impact of paper manufacturing has not received much attention in the graphic design community yet, but it is likely to become a much bigger deal in coming years.

The easiest thing designers can do to reduce the water consumed for the paper they use is to specify post-consumer recycled fiber. It takes significantly less water to repulp existing paper than it does to create virgin pulp from trees. On average, PCR fiber needs 42 percent less water compared with virgin fiber.

ENERGY ISSUES

When we burn fossil fuels, we release carbon dioxide into the atmosphere, which contributes to the greenhouse effect that is radically shifting our climate on a global scale. The paper industry burns a lot of fossil fuels to break down the lignin that binds wood fiber together and then to rapidly transform watery slurry into dry paper. Worldwide, the paper industry is an enormous emitter of greenhouse gases, rivaling the steel and chemical industries. That puts designers in a position to make a real difference by lowering our collective carbon footprint.

Designers can do two things to minimize the negative energy impacts from the paper they use:

- Use post-consumer recycled fiber (it requires a lot less energy), and

- Support renewable energy sources in paper making.

The u.s. Environmental Protection Agency estimates that manufacturing post-consumer recycled paper requires 64 percent less energy than manufacturing paper from virgin fiber.[11] That makes post-consumer recycled paper a triple positive, with benefits relating to fiber source, water usage, and energy.

After saving as much energy as possible, the next step is to figure out where the energy you do use comes from. Paper mills were traditionally powered by renewable hydroelectric power, and many mills still get a portion of their power from water turbines. But as energy requirements have increased, water power has become a smaller and smaller portion of the power mix industrywide. Mills increasingly rely on electricity from the power grid to run their paper machines. That electricity is largely generated by carbon-spewing power plants that burn natural gas and coal. Paper mills also rely on boilers to produce thermal energy in the form of steam used in drying the paper. Boilers are usually powered on-site by fuel oil, natural gas, or coal.

CHANGE IS IN THE WIND

Several leading manufacturers have made strides to change this carbon-intensive power profile in the past few years. In 2003, Mohawk Paper helped make energy a topic of conversation in the paper industry with a commitment to offset emissions from purchased electricity. Mohawk contracted to purchase Renewable Energy Certificates (RECs) equivalent to the output of one large wind turbine. That was enough to enable the company to market a few grades of paper as being "made with wind power." A few years later, the company increased its commitment to renewable energy by purchasing RECs to cover all of its electricity usage. Several other paper companies, including New Leaf Paper, Monadnock Paper, and Neenah Paper, have responded by offering paper grades made with renewable energy.

Electricity is just one part of the energy equation in making and distributing paper. Cleaning up the carbon footprint of paper also requires looking at the thermal energy used to dry the paper. This requires heat and steam, not electricity, so wind energy doesn't make sense here. Paper companies are using a variety of methods to neutralize the carbon emissions of all or part of their thermal energy usage. Mohawk purchased Verifiable

Emissions Reductions (VERS) to offset a portion of the fuel they burn to power their boilers. Neenah Paper powers some of its boilers in part by burning sludge filtered out of wastewater. New Leaf Paper promotes the use of "biogas," captured from a nearby landfill. Other mills are using waste heat from nearby power plants to reduce fossil fuel consumption.

These moves, combined with RECs that offset electricity consumption, have enabled Mohawk, Neenah and others to claim "carbon neutral" manufacturing processes for specific grades of paper. This does not account for carbon emissions relating to forestry, pulping, or transportation, but it is a step in the right direction. Full life-cycle carbon accounting is the next step on the carbon-cutting pathway. New Leaf Paper and Mohawk Paper are already moving in this direction by committing to use low-emissions biodiesel fuel in transportation. In an even bolder move, the Canadian forest products industry association pledged in late 2007 to achieve full life-cycle carbon neutrality for Canadian forest products, including paper, by 2015. That would include everything from logging operations, through pulp and paper manufacturing, all the way down to recycling and landfill. This is great news for designers, who now have an increasing range of climate-wise options to choose from.

Any "sustainable" solution for paper making must address fiber, energy, and water issues. Post-consumer fiber or agricultural waste should play a dominant role as a fiber source; chlorine and its derivatives should be eliminated from bleaching; water should be contained in a closed-loop manufacturing system; and energy from renewable sources should power the full life cycle of the product. But that doesn't mean that there is a single formula for sustainable paper. Two cutting edge mills illustrate very different approaches, both of which hold great promise.

The Danish mill Dalum Papir is located near Copenhagen and gets 70 percent of its fiber from regional urban recycling programs. The remaining fiber comes from FSC-certified forests. The mill has an integrated de-inking facility that uses enzymes to separate ink from fiber without harsh chemicals. This provides a steady supply of high-quality post-consumer fiber. In a classic example of "industrial ecology," Dalum has partnered with nearby cement manufacturers and power plants to find markets for the clays, fillers, and inks that are the by-products of de-inking so that nothing they receive goes to landfill. The de-inking facility bleaches pulp primarily with hydrogen peroxide, which eliminates toxic effluent problems. Water at the facility is typically reused six times before entering a biological treatment system. Energy for the mill comes primarily from an onsite boiler powered by wood chips rather than fossil fuels. Dalum represents the current state-of-the-art in recycled paper manufacturing.

On the other side of the globe, a company called Papyrus Australia is developing a very different model for sustainable paper manufacturing. The Papyrus technology transforms banana tree trunks, which are cut down annually after harvest, into paper in a low-energy process that requires no chemical inputs and no outside water supply. If development proceeds as planned, paper factories would be located near banana plantations and would create a valuable product from a waste material that currently is left to rot in the fields. The Papyrus technology is initially being targeted as a replacement for industrial paper and paperboard grades, but it may eventually yield a product that also competes well with premium-quality printing papers. Regardless of where it competes, though, it challenges us to think beyond the status quo for materials and manufacturing techniques.

Synthetic papers also hold great promise for the future. A variation on the current generation of synthetics would be a biopolymer paper that has two potential destinies: It could be recycled perpetually or composted whenever there is no return option. If the biopolymer were made from agricultural waste and in a process powered by renewable energy, then we'd have a truly exciting sustainable solution.

Another development worth watching is digital ink displays. New technologies from companies like E-Ink in Cambridge, Massachusetts, promise a paper-like user experience for dynamic content. The "digital paper display" uses little energy and can be refreshed millions of times. That could have a huge impact on how we publish our designs, especially for ephemeral media such as magazines, newspapers, and display graphics. Again, if done correctly, this could represent a better user experience with a much lower ecological footprint than that to which we are currently accustomed.

Specifying "green" paper is one of the simplest things a green graphic designer can do. It only requires knowledge and the will to break from the status quo. Environmentally improved paper is often a straight replacement for conventional virgin paper, and it does not require significant changes in manufacturing processes. Nonetheless, it can significantly reduce the ecological footprint of printed graphic design.

Specifying "green" paper is one of the simplest things a green graphic designer can do. It only requires knowledge and the will to break from the status quo.

ONE WORD:
PLASTICS

Like the internal combustion engine, plastics have enabled incredible advances in efficiency and quality of life over the past century. In the course of a few dozen years, plastics have become an essential part of our lives. They are often the lightest material available and can be energy efficient to manufacture. They can be clear or opaque, as well as flexible or rigid, and are adaptable to many design aesthetics. They can increase shelf life and reduce product spoilage. And, of course, plastics are often very cheap (at least from an initial economic cost perspective).

Yet, as with the internal combustion engine, petroleum-based plastics are currently pushing our society to the brink of ecological collapse. Plastics are made primarily from oil and natural gas, which are not renewable resources. In addition, by using fossil fuels for manufacturing and transport, plastics contribute to global warming. They often require toxic solvents and additives for their manufacturing processes. But the biggest problem with plastics is that they never go away. Nearly all of the molecules that have been pumping out of plastics factories for decades are still with us—and will remain with us for centuries. They litter the landscape and the oceans; they break into microscopic particles and enter the food chain. Like nuclear waste, plastic waste is a legacy that will outlive many generations of our children.

As designers, we need to weigh these negative and positive attributes of plastics as we decide which materials to use, and we need to search for ways to minimize the negative effects of the plastics that we choose to use. We need to use plastics in ways that preserve their material purity and prevent contamination of the natural environment over the very long term.

SYMBOLS OF CONFUSION

In a master stroke of deceptive communications, the Society of the Plastics Industry in 1988 appropriated the chasing arrow triangle, a universal symbol for recycling, as part of their system for labeling types of plastic resins. Consumers have been confused ever since. The symbol used on plastics **suggests** recycled content and real-world recyclability, yet it **means** something different. The symbol simply indicates which family of plastic resins a product or component is made of. **The suggestion of recycled content is completely false.** After two decades of miscommunication, plastics are by far the most likely material to be labeled with a "recycled" symbol, yet they are among the least likely materials to actually be recycled.

Here's what those symbols really mean, how the various resins are frequently used in packaging, and how they compare in terms of relative environmental impact[12]:

#1 POLYETHYLENE TEREPHTHALATE (PET)
bottles for water and soda, fiber for textiles

IMPACT: MODERATE (relatively high recycling rate, may contain toxic additives such as antimony trioxide)

#2 HIGH-DENSITY POLYETHYLENE (HDPE)
bottles for milk, juice, shampoo, liquid laundry detergent and motor oil, grocery bags, and cereal box liners

IMPACT: BETTER (low toxicity, relatively high recycling rate)

#3 POLYVINYL CHLORIDE (PVC)
clear films, most cling wraps, blister packs

IMPACT: WORST

#4 LOW-DENSITY POLYETHYLENE (LDPE)
bags for groceries, newspapers and garbage, some cling wraps, lids for containers

IMPACT: BETTER (low toxicity)

#5 POLYPROPYLENE (PP)
rigid containers for yogurt and deli foods, bottles for medicine and cosmetics

IMPACT: BETTER (low toxicity)

#6 POLYSTYRENE (PS)
CD jewel cases, takeout cups and food containers, foamed packing trays, foamed peanuts

IMPACT: BAD

#7 OTHER
indicates a less common resin type or a mix of more than one resin

IMPACT: BAD

PLASTIC PACKAGING RECYCLING RATES[13]

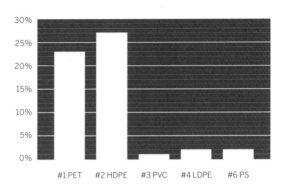

Only #2 HDPE or #1 PET have any realistic likelihood of being recycled in North America through municipal collection systems

If you are designing a plastic package, it's important to know that only #2 HDPE or #1 PET have any realistic likelihood of being recycled in North America through municipal collection systems. Approximately 23 percent of #1 PET soda and water bottles are recycled in the United States. #2 HDPE milk and juice containers are recycled roughly 27 percent of the time. The recycling rates for all other forms of plastic packaging are much lower. Any plastic packaging you specify will probably end up in a landfill. If it is not #1 or #2, that destiny is virtually guaranteed. The claim that plastics are "recyclable" is therefore not very meaningful in the real world. Recyclability is a good place to start, but it's not nearly enough.

There are several other design strategies worth considering for reducing the ecological impact of plastic packaging: considering biopolymers, selecting formulations that enable lightweighting, using post-consumer recycled content, and avoiding potentially toxic materials.

BIOPOLYMERS

Biopolymers, or bioplastics, are a broad group of materials made from natural resources that have physical characteristics similar to petroleum-based plastics. Many of the current biopolymers on the market are made from corn starch, which is processed into polylactic acid (PLA). Other biopolymers, such as polyhydroxyalkanoate (PHA), are made via microbial fermentation.

Biopolymers hold great promise for sustainable packaging because they maintain the functional advantages of petroleum plastics while offering two key advantages: They come from renewable resources, not fossil fuels, and they are typically biodegradable. Several factors have prevented biopolymers from being universally endorsed as an eco-packaging solution, but those barriers are gradually being resolved. The future, it seems, is in **bio**plastics.

Cost has long been a barrier to widespread adoption of biopolymers, but prices have come down in recent years because of process efficiencies. Meanwhile, rising oil prices have driven up the price of petroleum-based plastic, so the relative cost is much closer now.

The most popular biopolymers currently on the market are made from corn. Some of this corn is grown from genetically modified (GMO) seed. As a result, many companies in the natural foods industry, which might otherwise embrace biopolymer packaging, have steered clear. To address this problem, biopolymer producer NatureWorks began in 2005 offering an "identity-preserved" product line that allows packagers to specify a particular source for the corn. Newman's Own packages organic salad mix in containers made from non-GMO NatureWorks biopolymer. The program is limited to large volume customers, but that may change as demand increases.

One criticism of biopolymers is that they remove corn from the food supply. The same can be said of ethanol fuel. Researchers are working on ways to make biopolymers from agricultural waste such as corn husks rather than food crops. Others are trying to make biopolymers from cow manure, orange peels, chicken feathers, and smoke-stack gases. In theory, nearly any cheap source of carbon could be used as a feedstock for biopolymers. This development could further minimize the ecological and economic impacts of biopolymers. This research, however, has not yet been widely commercialized.

Another current issue with biopolymers is where to compost them. Some municipal composters won't accept biopolymers that do not break down within a specified period. These composters turn yard waste and food into compost that they sell. Customers buying compost do not want to see a partially composted fork or other bits of "plastic" when they spread the compost in their gardens. Industrial composters are working with the bioplastics manufacturers to make the bioplastics compatible with the composters' requirements.

Several manufacturers have developed petroleum plastics with natural starch or mineral additives that enable the plastic to "break down" or "photodegrade" but not to fully biodegrade. This may result in a material that uses **less** petroleum than conventional plastics, but it may also make it easier for the remaining plastic molecules to disperse in the environment and enter the food chain. These partially biodegradable plastics also confuse consumers and can contaminate municipal compost systems.

Finally, biopolymers present new challenges for plastics recyclers. Because they look the same as conventional plastics, recyclers fear that their already-difficult job of separating plastics by type will become virtually impossible. According to NatureWorks, PLA can be identified and separated from a mixed-waste stream using readily available scanning equipment. The company has developed a buy-back program to encourage a post-consumer market for PLA.

As designers and biopolymer manufacturers overcome these obstacles, it becomes possible to imagine a revolutionary green packaging system. Designers could soon specify, "annually renewable, carbon neutral, biodegradable, recyclable, cost effective, lightweight packaging based on organic agriculture practices and agricultural waste products." Quite a mouthful, to be sure, but this represents a potential win-win-win solution for ecology, economics, and design innovation.

LIGHTWEIGHTING

The Oregon Department of Environmental Quality commissioned a large life-cycle assessment study analyzing twenty-six packaging solutions for shipping nonfragile goods such as clothing. The study concluded that the most important factor in determining the overall environmental impact of a package is the weight of the materials used.[14] Lightweight, flexible bags had a much smaller total environmental impact than corrugated paper boxes—even if the boxes were made from recycled fiber. Bags have two big advantages over boxes: they use much less material, and they ship more compactly. The reduced impact is surprisingly consistent for levels of energy use, solid waste, greenhouse gas emissions, and air and water pollution.

Choosing post-consumer recycled content usually lowers the environmental impact of a package, but this is a smaller-scale improvement than choosing a lightweight material. One of the recommendations from the Oregon study is, "Once you've chosen a packaging material, it typically makes good environmental sense to try and maximize the level of post-consumer recycled content. However, be wary of choosing a packaging material only because it contains high levels of post-consumer recycled content."

The Oregon study looked at one specific packaging challenge, but other analysts have reached similar conclusions for other types of packaging. **Stonyfield Farm** is a major seller of organic yogurt and milk products and has long been a leader in green business circles. Their yogurt is packaged in #5 polypropylene (PP) tubs that are not easily recyclable in North America. The decision to use PP was based on research showing that "less than 5 percent of the total environmental cost of packaging is in the disposal. Over 95 percent of the environmental cost is in the production of the package—in the energy used and toxins created in the manufacturing process." Stonyfield Farm chose #5 PP plastic over #2 HDPE mainly because they were able to make a significantly lighter container with PP. In order to address the recyclability issue, Stonyfield Farms developed a take-back program and a partnership with Recycline, which manufactures toothbrushes and razors from recycled yogurt containers. Only a tiny percentage of the containers produced are actually recycled this way, but it does open a path toward a better destiny for the package.

Stonyfield Farm and **Recycline** have teamed up to make toothbrushes and razor handles from recycled yogurt tubs.

Aveda Cosmetics is a leader in using post-consumer recycled plastic packaging.

POST-CONSUMER RECYCLED CONTENT

Using post-consumer recycled (PCR) plastic is one way to reduce the ecological impact of conventional plastic packaging. Several companies have been pushing the state-of-the-art for PCR packaging over the past several years. **Aveda Cosmetics** now uses 80 percent–100 percent post-consumer recycled content in its plastic bottles. According to John Delfausse, Aveda's Vice President of Packaging, they have managed to integrate the recycled content at no extra cost and no compromise on quality.

Several high-tech companies have also embraced recycled plastic packaging. Logitech and Motorola have both used recycled PET blister packs called EnviroShell from Winterborne, Inc., in California.

It is a common misconception that recycled plastics are never allowed for food packaging. This was the case years ago, but the U.S. Food and Drug Administration has updated its regulations and has issued a "favorable opinion on the suitability of a specific process for producing post-consumer recycled

(PCR) plastic to be used in the manufacturing of food-contact articles." That means that it's now possible to specify up to 100 percent PCR plastic packaging, even for food-contact uses. Pheonix Technologies in Ohio is one manufacturer that produces high-quality, food-contact approved PET resin from 100 percent post-consumer feedstock.

AVOIDING TOXICITY

Avoiding toxicity is another important part of minimizing the ecological impact of plastic packaging. The most obvious step is to avoid anything labeled #3 PVC or "vinyl." PVC is widely believed to be toxic to human and environmental health in its manufacture, use, and disposal. It is often called the "poison plastic." [12] Many countries and municipalities have begun to tightly regulate its use despite fierce lobbying by the vinyl industry. Several major corporations have also committed to phasing out PVC in products and packaging.

It can be difficult for designers to avoid PVC in certain applications. The retail and trade show **signage industry**, for instance, is almost entirely built around vinyl materials. The main options offered by signage fabricators include vinyl applied letters, PVC Sintra® board substrates, vinyl printed banners, and large-format inkjet prints on adhesive-backed vinyl. Also, fabricators often charge extra to use materials that are unfamiliar to them. There are alternatives, but it requires research and creativity to find and use them if you are working with a limited budget.

When Celery designed a signage system for Elephant Pharmacy, we specified a wide variety of nonvinyl solutions. Some of the wall signs were made of laser-cut plywood letters, which were stained dark blue. The wooden letters were then mounted to the wall with aluminum "stand-offs." It's possible to laser-cut any number of materials to create interesting dimensional letters.

Instead of using rigid pvc board for many of the signs at Elephant, we used flexible banners. Some of these were printed on cotton canvas. Other banners were printed on EcoSpun® recycled PET plastic fabric. Banner Creations in Minneapolis prints banners with die-sublimation technology, which emits fewer volatile organic compounds (vocs) than inkjet printers, and they frequently work with EcoSpun canvas.

We were not able to completely eliminate vinyl from the Elephant store. The hanging signs in the store are made from bamboo plywood, but the applied letters are vinyl. We designed large murals for the walls, and found artists to hand paint them, but this would have taken more than a week to install and would have required scaffolding in the aisles of the store. We did not have time for this, so the murals were printed on adhesive-backed vinyl and installed in a few hours.

Celery has continued researching alternative substrate materials and printing techniques so that future signage projects may completely eliminate vinyl. Sonoma Graphic Products recently released several substrates made from recycled paper for indoor and exterior display graphics applications. Their x-board and Mondi Xtreme panels are designed for use with flat-bed inkjet printers. Combine this with a uv-curable inkjet printer

ONE WORD: PLASTICS

(no VOC emissions) such as those from MacDermid Colorspan or Inca, and you've got a far less toxic solution than the standard fare.

Other non-PVC substrates for display graphics include Di-Bond®, which is a polystyrene sheet sandwiched between two layers of aluminum, and Structa-Board®, which is polystryrene foam faced with wood fiber. Circle Graphics produces a wide-format banner material called Eco-Flexx, which is made of polyethylene and is touted as having a recycling program in place.

Credit cards are another industry dominated by vinyl. Nearly all credit cards and smart cards are made from PVC plastic. But less toxic options are starting to arrive on the market. The Co-operative Bank and Barclay's Bank both recently released credit cards in the United Kingdom made from #1 PETG film. The discount retailer Target recently released a gift card made of Mirel™, a biopolymer manufactured by Telles™. Unlike many other biopolymers, Mirel decomposes in a home compost pile.

Toxicologists have raised serious concerns in recent years about the harmful effects of **antimony**, which is a heavy metal often used as a catalyst in manufacturing PET plastic. In response, resin manufacturers such as Zimmer (ecocat) and Wellman (PermaClearTi) now offer antimony-free PET resin.

Polycarbonate (PC) is one of the "#7 other" resins. It contains a chemical called bisphenol-a (BPA), which has been shown to disrupt the endocrine system of laboratory animals. Since polycarbonate is frequently used for baby bottles, there has been a great debate in recent years about whether BPA can leach into food carried in polycarbonate containers. In 2008, the Canadian government banned the use of plastics containing BPA for baby bottles. Other governments are likely to follow Canada's lead. Until less toxic forms of polycarbonate are developed, designers should avoid the material for applications that contact food, especially if the package might be heated in a microwave oven.

Plastic packaging is a complex and often counterintuitive topic for green designers. Experts who conduct sophisticated life-cycle assessments consistently advocate for lightweight, flexible plastic packaging. Because they require less energy for manufacturing and transport, experts say, these packages are typically the best available option. Meanwhile, reputable scientists also warn of dangerous environmental toxicity and the pervasiveness of plastic particles in our food chain.

Most of available options, it seems, just aren't good enough. Designers want nontoxic, lightweight, low energy, inexpensive, versatile materials to work with. Until such materialsare readily available, green designers must rely on ingenuity and a series of measured compromises.

DESIGN FOR CHANG

The greatest impact of graphic design doesn't lie in the materials we use. All the paper and printing we specify and all the energy we burn in transit definitely add up to a significant impact on the world. But our real impact lies in our ability to communicate, persuade, and ultimately to change how audiences act. At its core, being a designer is about being an agent for change. Being a green designer is about being an agent for **positive change**.

Graphic designers effect change by helping clients communicate. The problem is that we are typically empowered to worry about **how** to communicate but not **what** to communicate. In the real world, though, there's rarely a clear line between the how and the what. The end user perceives an integrated brand experience. It's just a big ripe design avocado—the medium and the message are one.

In most cases, the messages we work with are defined "upstream" from the designer. They are born out of business strategies, brand strategies, or marketing strategies before the designer is engaged on a project. These messages—which are at the very core of what we do and largely determine the impact we have on the world—can often seem beyond the reach of graphic design. They are not actually out of our reach, but we may need to learn how to grab hold of them.

DESIGN ACTIVISM

The most obvious way that graphic designers can actively define the messages we work with is by choosing our clients. For instance, we can help clients promote practices or products that help people lead healthier, more sustainable lives. We can help clients educate the public—and spur them to take action—about social and environmental problems and solutions. Many designers do a certain amount of pro bono work for social and environmental causes, but this type of design need not be restricted to a sideline. A growing number of designers have built thriving consultancies by primarily or exclusively serving nonprofits, foundations, public agencies, and green businesses. That is how Celery started ten years ago. Since then, we have worked with dozens of advocacy groups and values-based businesses large and small. We have learned a great deal from our clients, and because of them, we have had many opportunities to deliver inspiring, important messages.

By collaborating with organizations that we truly believe in, we align our own values with the values of our clients—our cause and their cause are the same. This is different from the typical fee-for-service model, which is driven exclusively by financial "value." Green design unleashes the power of extended self-interest. The designer can be an active citizen and a professional at the same time. This is design activism, and it's a completely viable (and fulfilling) way to make a living and build a career

GREEN BRANDING

Green branding is a form of design activism. Designers help companies articulate the values that give them purpose, then use those values as a framework for communications. This helps define the company in terms that most people can relate to. It humanizes large organizations and shines a spotlight on some purpose beyond profit. The designer collaborates with marketers and green business strategists to reach the intended audiences on an emotional level.

The brand helps companies build relationships with their audiences, of course, but it also helps companies know how to act. Branding is largely about projection—what values you are projecting through your communications—but the process of developing and managing a green brand also involves a great deal of reflection. Business managers are forced to look critically at their companies and identify any actions and policies that may contradict or denigrate their core values.

Lots of companies focus on values in order to craft a "mission statement." The statement then hangs in a picture frame on the wall somewhere and gets dusted off once a year when it's time to publish an annual report. Mission statements are high-level, abstract documents. It's hard to make a mission statement meaningful to the vast majority of employees, much less to a company's customers. As you move away from the core circle of executives that participated in crafting the mission, it becomes progressively more dogmatic and less relevant to the day-to-day reality of running a business. Green brands help to remedy this by pulling the values down off the wall and stitching them into the fabric of communications that employees engage in every day. It makes them accessible, so that every decision and customer touch point can be viewed through the lens of company values.

Effective green branding is built on three pillars:

1 GREENER PROGRAMS AND PRODUCTS. A company needs to demonstrate real leadership on several fronts and show that it understands its impacts and is actively working to reduce them. This leadership does not need to include every aspect of a business or every niche player in the market, but the leadership must be genuine—a collection of moderately less bad products is unlikely to build a strong green brand.

2 CLEARLY ARTICULATED VALUES AND A VISION FOR SUSTAINABILITY. Companies need to have an understanding of the material issues, a willingness to go beyond the status quo, and the humility to resist over-statement. This is difficult to achieve unless they've established a vision for the future that includes ambitious sustainability goals and values.

3 A STRONG COMMUNICATIONS CAMPAIGN. Companies need to find creative ways to effectively communicate their green messages and break through the clutter of competing claims.

Eco Innovation
Sun Microsystems

Traditional marketing sets the company versus its competitors in terms such that the company comes out on top. Green branding positions a company versus the ideal of sustainability, knowing full well that the company will fall short. This is less crazy than it sounds, because few competitors perform well either. The competition is then waged on who has the most compelling vision, thought leadership, and values—and who can continue to demonstrate innovative solutions.

Celery recently had an opportunity to put these principles into practice by helping Sun Microsystems develop the Sun Eco Innovation brand identity. For many years, Sun has been an environmental leader in many aspects of high tech and enterprise computing. Our challenge was to show the connections between a wide array of subjects such as super-efficient computer servers, an impressive work-from-home program (more than half of Sun's employees telecommute at least part time), and software applications that allow datacenters to get more processing power without adding hardware. Rather than any single product line or program, Sun is really distinguished by a "do more with less" ethos that has led to environmental innovation across many aspects of its business.

At the same time, executives at Sun readily acknowledge that the company's operations and products still cause significant environmental damage. So we wanted to communicate Sun's environmental leadership without diminishing the importance of the challenges that lie ahead.

The resulting Sun Eco Innovation brand signifier is a top-tier brand element, meaning that it expresses company values and relates to the corporation's highest-level brand promise. The brand is used whenever Sun communicates about environmental initiatives or promotes products and services that offer clear environmental advantages. It is **not** a product attribute, label, or certification scheme. Eco Innovation is essentially a messaging motif that coordinates the disparate environmental activities across the company.

It was very important to Sun and Celery that we clarify how the Eco Innovation should and shouldn't be implemented. We developed a three-part usage framework similar to Celery's Sustainability Scorecard. SEE PAGE 186. The "green" zone lists subject areas and product groups that make up Sun's primary proof points for environmental leadership. These should always be accompanied by the Eco Innovation brand. The "yellow" zone explains when to use the brand with other products and services, on the basis of demonstrable environmental benefit and messaging priorities (use the brand only if there's a clear green message). The "red" zone explains when the brand should not be used, including all communications where an environmental benefit is not a top messaging priority or isn't clearly demonstrated. The goal of this system is to build strong recognition of Sun's eco-activities, maintain the authenticity of the brand, and avoid inappropriate environmental claims.

AVOIDING THE GREENWASH TRAP

Green brands tell the world that ethical and environmental values are important metrics of the business' success. If a company's actions contradict the values they promote, then the brand suffers. Green branding opens companies up to charges of "greenwashing" if they overpromote and under-perform. Critics and competitors are often happy to draw attention to those contradictions when a green brand isn't backed up by a legitimate green business action.

Most business people believe that they have strong values, but they often lack the perspective to identify contradictions when their actions don't live up to those values. Companies fall into greenwashing when everyone in the chain of communication "drinks the Kool-Aid" and uncritically accepts the legitimacy of company actions and statements. This ultimately leaves the company vulnerable to being blindsided by outside critics who point out the contradictions between brand and action.

Since design stands between business strategy and audience impact, graphic designers can play an important role as gate-keepers in preventing greenwashing. We act as brand stewards, and we can call attention to contradictions—in the name of protecting the brand—before damaging messages get published.

Green brand stewards can focus on three key factors:

Authenticity is a measure of how well the values that a company projects align with the reality of the company's actions —and therefore how believable the brand is. Authenticity sits squarely in the realm of communications. As stewards of authenticity, designers can prevent superficial, vague, or unsubstantiated green statements, not to mention unsustainable printing materials.

Restraint is a matter of preventing harmful exaggeration. No company is truly sustainable, and few processes or products are really "environmentally friendly." Yet marketers with limited understanding of environmental issues find exaggeration hard to resist. Relatively minor accomplishments are often taken out of context and clustered together to give the impression that a company is more "green" than it actually is. Over time, exaggeration dampens the potency of a green brand. Strong green brands are built on vision, smart communications, and demonstrable progress. As brand stewards, designers can help prevent excessive background noise caused by irrelevant or exaggerated green claims.

Follow-through is a matter of articulating strategies to deliver on the green brand promise. Brand communication is a promise to audiences. As designers, we help companies make the promises and can also help companies imagine ways to fulfill their promises. In essence, we harness a company's desire to seem more green than it actually is and use that to drive real changes in the way the company operates. It won't happen instantaneously, but designers who help companies develop green brands are perfectly positioned to influence what goes into the development pipeline. We can encourage greener products, services, and practices in the name of delivering on the brand promise.

TerraChoice, an environmental market research company, recently surveyed over one thousand products that make various eco claims. The company found that almost none of the products thoroughly and clearly backed up their claims. On the basis of this research, Terrachoice identified "The Six Sins of Greenwashing." These are:

1 SIN OF THE HIDDEN TRADE-OFF: making a green claim based on a very narrow set of criteria, thereby masking negative environmental impacts from other aspects of the product. These claims may not be technically false claims, but customers feel deceived when they learn about broader impacts.

2 SIN OF NO PROOF: making a green claim without providing clear access to supporting information. Companies essentially say "trust us," which is not good enough for long-term brand building.

3 SIN OF VAGUENESS: making a claim that is so vague that it's meaningless. In lieu of significant proof points, companies often end up with a lot of vague statements like "we care" and "environmentally friendly" and "doing our part to protect the Earth." These are all poorly defined claims that set the bar too low to offer any useful differentiation.

4 SIN OF IRRELEVANCE: making a claim that suggests environmental benefit but is actually unhelpful to customers seeking environmentally beneficial products. This includes "taking credit" for attributes that are legally required or are common within a product category.

5 SIN OF LESSER OF TWO EVILS: making claims of relative benefit within a product category while ignoring the weakness of the category as a whole. This phenomenon is also known as "The Tallest of the Dwarves" marketing.

6 SIN OF FIBBING: making claims that are simply false. This is far less common than other sins, but it opens a company up to direct legal liability.

By taking an active role in crafting messages, designers can help clients avoid greenwashing. On the other hand, if designers are not conscious of the risks involved, we may inadvertently become accomplices to the crime.

Ultimately, the pervasiveness of greenwashing in popular media is an indication that consumer values are changing. Hunter Lovins, who cofounded the well-respected environmental nonprofit Rocky Mountain Institute, recently shocked many environmentalists by stating, "I think greenwashing is good." [15] Lovins puts it this way:

> Hypocrisy is the first step to real change. If a company makes a claim about something, then you can hold them accountable, and as they make small steps to bring their performance in line with what they're marketing, to avoid a backlash for greenwashing, they actually see the benefit of that improved performance, and it becomes something they integrate into their business for real.

TRANSPARENCY AND TRANSFORMATIVE COMMUNICATION

The best antidote to greenwashing is transparency. Old models of corporate communication, which crafted a flawless façade for companies by tightly controlling the release of information, don't work so well in a world of grassroots bloggers and instantaneous Google searches. A single persistent critic with a bit of demonstrable evidence can now gain as much visibility as any corporate communications campaign formulated by a PR firm.

It's important to remember that sustainability is not some vague, malleable notion. It is specific and measurable. It is also incredibly rare. Truly sustainable solutions are usually an ambition rather than a reality. Smart companies acknowledge this. They define a vision for sustainability, set measurable goals, and then craft messages that educate their audiences about the journey they are on. Sophisticated customers tend to respect this honesty and respect such careful companies; we have all been disappointed too many times to buy the "we're perfect" marketing pitch.

Smart companies are now embracing a different model of corporate communications based on openness and the free flow of information. It turns out that the world doesn't come crashing down when companies talk honestly about the environmental and social challenges that they face. When companies confront difficult issues and engage with their critics, they earn the respect and trust of skeptical audiences.

Transparency helps graphic designers craft communications with real substance. It takes design out of the role of cheerleading and places it into a role of change agent. Designers can help simplify, clarify complex issues, and educate audiences about the path companies are on. We can help build compelling stories from real performance and plans.

CORPORATE RESPONSIBILITY

Corporate social responsibility (CSR) reports have developed over the past decade into the premier forum for corporate transparency about environmental and social issues. CSR is an acknowledgment that companies need to do more than make a profit in order to earn the trust, respect, and business of customers. They must answer to the "triple bottom line" of financial, social, and environmental performance. This may come in response to pressure from advocacy groups or companies may simply see that expectations for transparency are changing.

Celery has collaborated on many major reports in print and on the Web over the past several years, and we have worked through many challenges along the way. Some of the key lessons we have learned are:

Tell an interesting story. The first rule of good design is that it must be effective. If the intended audience does not read a communications piece, then the whole effort is a waste. Designers can add value to reports by developing visual narratives that draw readers into the information. A coherent concept or storyline can help transform a dry compliance document into an engaging communications piece. A clear, skimmable visual hierarchy can make it approachable.

Integrate and extend the brand. CSR reports communicate brand values. However, a report's messages and objectives differ from most other corporate communications. One of the challenges in designing a successful report is to build a bridge between the main brand promise and the specific CSR priorities of the organization. If designed well, a CSR report adds value and builds trust in the parent brand. If designed poorly, a CSR report can seem like a "greenwash" or seem detached from the "real" business.

Strike the right tone. The tone of a CSR report must balance between a company's marketing and sales objectives and the need for transparency, authenticity, and honesty in reporting. Every company hopes that its CSR efforts will help establish it as a responsible—or at least a benign—corporate citizen. Yet reports that send the a message of "look at how great we are" generally are met with skepticism in the public. Good design is one of the main ways to successfully strike that balance.

Make a point. CSR reports attempt to convey large quantities of data without putting audiences to sleep. Designers can focus on information design in order to bring the data to life. Like a sentence or a paragraph, a chart or graph should clearly convey some message. What is the "take away" message of a particular graph? It may be, *"There's basically no change from last year"* or *"European growth has been the real driver of change."* Good information design can ensure that readers understand the intended message in the data.

CSR reports are an important piece of external brand communications for many organizations, but they can also help to transform the internal dynamics within the companies that publish them. First, they encourage companies to compete on environmental and social metrics. Competition is a powerful motivator for the business world, and it causes huge organizations to change course very quickly. Secondly, CSR reports give employees permission to bring their values to work. A meaningful report provides affirmation for a lot of people who would like to change the status quo but struggle to break from the past. This, too, can unleash a flurry of rapid change within the organization. When viewed over several reporting cycles, it is often easy to see a shift in how reporting companies manage their business and how they manage their brands.

TOOLS FOR CHANGE

Viewed in this light, a CSR report is really a tool for change. A green brand is also a tool for change. Both of these change the way outsiders perceive organizations, and they also change how the people who make up the organization perceive themselves—and ultimately how they act.

This gets to the seed at the center of the "design avocado." When designing tools for change, the designer can play an important role in identifying the desired outcome and crafting creative strategies to achieve that outcome. This puts all the stuff we use and the artifact we create in proper context. It is a means to an end, not an end in itself. We are really trying to change the world for the better, and graphic designers are empowered to be multimedia change agents, using whatever strategies best drive that change.

A great example of this is the Seafood Watch wallet card. Jim Ales and his team of designers at the Monterey Bay Aquarium have created a simple, effective (and beautiful) tool that empowers smarter choices at the dinner table and the grocery store. The card is laid out in three easy-to-read columns: Best choices, Good Alternatives, and Avoid. The first column lists fisheries that are being sustainably harvested. The third column contains a list of fisheries that are endangered. And the middle column shows fisheries that fall somewhere in between. This is truly design activism—a solution that simplifies complex issues and enables positive change.

The Monterey Bay Aquarium's **Seafood Watch Wallet Card** is a great example of design for change. It transforms complex information into a form that is easy to use in a restaurant or fish market.

PUTTING IT
INTO PRACTICE

When we put green design into practice, there's no clear line
of demarcation between such things as "design for destiny,"
"design for shipping," and "establishing authenticity." We
give names to each of these things in order to explain them,
but they don't really happen in isolation. "Design Backwards"
is just a tool to help us look downstream at the full production process and user experience. And "Design for Change"

is a device that reminds us to be active upstream in crafting strategies and messages. In practice, though, these all merge into a fluid creative process. A challenge in one phase inspires a solution in another. Each new production method, client request, material selection, and aesthetic choice cascades through the project and influences other choices. This is what holistic design looks like.

Lemnis Lighting offers an illustration of this. Lemnis is a Dutch company that manufactures state-of-the-art LED light bulbs. The bulbs use 90 percent less energy than comparable incandescent bulbs and nearly half the energy of compact fluorescent (CFL) bulbs. They also last thirty-five years (eight times longer than fluorescents) and don't contain toxic mercury. It's a revolutionary product with a huge environmental benefit. It's also expensive. Over the long run, each bulb saves its owner something like $250, but first someone must invest $25 to buy it. That is a lot of money up front compared with $1.50 for a standard incandescent or even $6 for an "energy efficient" CFL.

It is a good design challenge to communicate to buyers that a $25 light bulb is a wise investment for them and for the environment. Celery started the project with a wide-ranging brand exploration and holistic design process. We designed downstream, upstream, backwards, and upside-down.

One of our first realizations was that a $25 light bulb shouldn't be presented like a $1 light bulb. This is a radically different (and better) technology, and the user experience should reflect that. So, instead of garish colors and countless violators, the Lemnis package is clean and refined, with lots of white space and soothing ambient imagery.

The shape we settled on is a truncated pyramid. This shape stands out on the shelf and fits snugly to the bulb inside. The name of the bulb is Pharox, for the lighthouse that was one of the Seven Wonders of the Ancient World, and the pyramid shape references that. It also nests nicely in shipping containers, which makes it a pretty good "design for shipping" solution. We specified 100 percent post-consumer recycled paper for the package and worked out the dieline so that boxes could fit efficiently 6-up on a press sheet (design for manufacturing). The box also folds up and locks without any adhesives, which makes it eminently recyclable (design for destiny).

This all adds up to a very unique package for a light bulb, but we also thought about the brand experience beyond the store shelf. We imagined all the potential fates for this package other than the trash heap or the recycle bin. We decided that the best possible fate would keep the package close to the bulb it was designed to hold. So we designed the box so that buyers

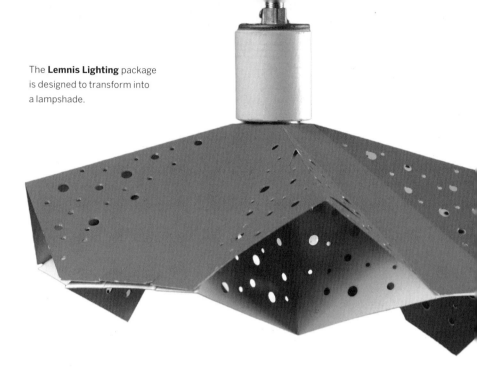

The **Lemnis Lighting** package is designed to transform into a lampshade.

could unfold it, turn it inside-out, and use the package itself as a lamp shade. A free gift, a nice story, and a profoundly different brand experience for this new technology.

None of this was planned in advance. We simply opened ourselves to a full range of influences and let the creativity flow. The design process changed the final design, of course, but it also changed the way Lemnis thought about packaging. Instead of being a cost item and a surface for messages, the package became a source of value and real brand differentiation. Obviously, the pyramid box is more expensive than a standard rectangular box used for incandescents or the plastic blister packs used for compact fluorescents—despite the manufacturing efficiencies we designed. But it's not more expensive as a percentage of the bulb's cost, and it offers real differentiation in the market and long-lasting brand value.

TRANSFORMATIONAL GREEN DESIGN:
HEWLETT PACKARD'S GLOBAL CITIZENSHIP REPORT

Hewlett Packard's Global Citizenship Report offers a very different example of green design. For several years, Celery has worked with HP to shift their reporting from a large printed document to a robust online presentation supported by a host of smaller, more targeted materials. Rather than a radical reinvention that happens all at once, the HP report has been transformed over the course of several years in a steady march. The end result, though, is a significantly "dematerialized" solution. SEE PAGE 98.

On the face of it, the shift away from big printed reports sounds easy. Many companies publish reports as Acrobat PDF files and put the files on their Web sites. However, the download time puts a barrier between the user and the content, which impedes the user experience. Also, many people prefer not to read long documents on computer screens so they hit the "Print" button and end up with a stack of single-sided pages coming out of a relatively inefficient office printer. Ironically, large downloadable reports may use more paper and energy than commercial printing and publishing; it's just externalized to the user.

Our solution has been to create a Web-native report for HP. It is more immediately accessible and enables readers to browse the full report without printing it. Over the years, we've added more sophisticated interface elements and Web-based tools that could never be replicated in print. Many viewers still print from the Web in order to read long documents, but the content is segmented, so they are unlikely to print the full report.

In 2006, we developed a tool that enables users to assemble their own "custom" reports from the sections that interest them.

We also created a twenty page customer report, which drives traffic to the Web version for more information. The shorter length makes it possible to "localize" the content for many different languages and regions (HP published nineteen targeted versions in 2007). It also makes distributed, on-demand digital printing more viable.

Finally, for events that draw customers from several countries, we created a single international CD-ROM disc containing all of the localized overview brochures. We housed the disc in a unique package—a paperboard cover with a tray made from foamed cellulose (a product called PaperFoam). Since the tray is made of cellulose, it is fully recyclable with the paper cover. It makes for a unique, lightweight package that demonstrates HP's commitment to leadership in the area of corporate responsibility.

HP's **Global Citizenship Report** was published in several languages on a CD-ROM. The case was made of recycled paper on recyclable PaperFoam.

Much of the discussion in this book has focused on printed communications and hybrids of print and Web publishing. However, green design is equally relevant to pure web design. In fact, with the "stuff" of printed communications out of the way, web designers may be able to focus more attention on designing for change.

OpenEco.org is a web-based tool that allows companies to calculate and track greenhouse gas emissions and then compare performance and best practices with other members of the OpenEco community. Sun Microsystems sponsored the project to develop a tool that could easily manage the emissions from their hundreds of facilities, but they quickly decided to make the tool available online for free. Natural Logic advised on the structure and methodology behind the tool, Code Magi engineered the tool, and Celery designed the identity and user interface. The goal was to create an easy-to-use tool for doing sophisticated calculations.

OpenEco is interesting in that it brings slick user interface design and programming to an arena that has suffered from a severe lack of user-friendly tools. But more importantly, the tool empowers companies of any scale to better understand the impacts of their operations. Creating a greenhouse gas audit can be an expensive and time-consuming process, but OpenEco is free and it allows companies to see results after just a few hours. The design is essential in making the tool accessible to a wide array of users—from beginners to professional specialists.

The same could be said about a host of innovative web-based businesses. ZipCar, which runs a successful car-sharing business in many cities in North America, would not be successful were it not for the company's easy-to-use online user interface. In a sense, good design makes this eco-innovative business possible. Likewise, Apple's smart interface design for the iTunes Store makes possible a music and video distribution system with a relatively tiny environmental footprint.

The Web is also fertile ground for designers engaging in direct social activism. For example, Free Range Studios has designed a string of wildly successful web-based animations that advocate for a variety of progressive causes. *The Meatrix* educates viewers about the problems associated with factory farming. *The Story of Stuff* helps to illuminate our unhealthy patterns of consumption. These little Web movies have been downloaded by millions of viewers and have helped to spur serious public dialogue about the issues they address.

In each of these examples, designs for virtual experiences are driving real-world behavioral change. This is a potent form of "design for change." In all likelihood, Web user interface design will play a major role in the development of green design as a whole.

BEYOND SUSTAINABILITY

Values-based branding and corporate responsibility reporting both represent an expansion of what it means to be a successful business. It's no longer enough to earn a profit and not break the law. Companies must be net contributors to society in order to earn the respect of peers and customers. Green design is the creative corollary to these movements. The old definition of "good" design simply fails to satisfy the needs of our times. Real goodness goes beyond the aesthetics of the designed artifact and encompasses the making of that artifact, the content that it delivers and the impact it has on society.

We have an opportunity to transform the way design gets made—to forge an industry that respects the limits of our planet and contributes net value to society. More importantly, graphic designers have a key role to play in the broader transformation to sustainable economies.

Ultimately, "sustainability" is just a beginning. We don't want to sustain. We want to thrive. It is extremely important that we transform our communications systems to cause far less environmental damage. But being "less bad" is not what motivates us. We are motivated by the exciting, creative opportunities that await us. We strive for the positive potential that designers can unleash—in our own practice, in the operations of our clients, and in the actions of the people who receive our messages.

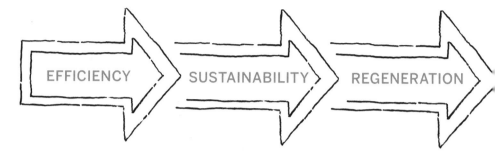

EFFICIENCY SUSTAINABILITY REGENERATION

Designers are enablers. Our impact goes far beyond the physical stuff that we use and specify. It encompasses the messages we convey and the actions we inspire. Green design challenges us to embrace this broadened definition of design and use it for the benefit of us all. We live in an exciting, creative time of transformation, with very big problems that demand solutions—both big and small. Designers are perfectly poised to offer substantive solutions. But it means that we must shake up the status quo. We need to think clearly about the change that we hope to achieve, and devise strategies that fulfill that potential. In order to design for change, we must change the way we design.

Unless someone like you, cares a whole awful lot, nothing's going to get better. It's not.

DR. SEUSS, *The Lorax*

	SOURCE	ENERGY IMPACTS	DESTINY
PREFERRED +	Made from sustainably harvested, renewable resource; no known toxicity	Made with renewable energy; very moderate embodied energy	Fully recyclable; fully compostable; reusable
CAUTION	Made from conventional renewable resource	Made with nonrenewable energy; low embodied energy	Compatible with incineration
AVOID	Made from nonrenewable resource; known toxic impacts	Made with nonrenewable energy; high embodied energy	Requires conventional or hazardous waste landfill

PAPER

PAPER	SOURCE	ENERGY	DESTINY
Post-consumer recycled fiber			
Pre-consumer recycled fiber			
FSC certified virgin fiber			
Conventional virgin fiber			
Alternative agricultural fiber			
Agricultural waste fiber			
Plastic laminated paper			
TCF/PCF bleaching			
ECF bleaching			
"Wind-powered" paper			

PLASTICS

PLASTICS	SOURCE	ENERGY	DESTINY
#1 PET			
#2 HDPE			
#3 PVC			
#4 LDPE			
#5 PP			
#6 PS			
#7 Other Plastics			
Biopolymers (non-GMO)			
Biopolymers (GMO)			

This is an abridged version of Celery's Sustainability Scorecard at the time of this writing. It is included here to serve as a framework and a starting point for assessing which materials and processes represent the best choice in any particular situation. It is not intended as an exhaustive or authoritative guide.

INKS

INKS	SOURCE	ENERGY	DESTINY
Petroleum inks	▬		
Vegetable inks	▬		
CMYK pigments	▬		
Most spot pigments	▬		
Metal-containing spot pigments	▬		▬
Metallic pigments	▬		▬
Varnish	▬		
Aqueous coating			
UV inks			
Foil stamping	▬		▬

BINDERY

BINDERY	SOURCE	ENERGY	DESTINY
Mechanical bind (saddle stitch)	▬		▬
Mechanical bind (singer stitch)	▬		▬
Perfect bind (PUR hot melt)			
Perfect bind (EVA hot melt)			
Starch adhesive	▬	▬	▬

The following spot color inks contain relatively high levels of metals. SEE PAGE 113.

PMS #	Parts Per Million		PMS #	Parts Per Million	
	Barium	Copper		Barium	Copper
123	18	2	347	8	2376
137	25	2	354	64	2680
1375	32	2	361	10	1426
151	39	2	368	10	952
1585	60	2	389	15	207
165	67	2	419	19	828
1655	81	2	438	93	2063
172	94	2	445	88	2475
Warm Red	122	1	450	31	937
1788	118	1	457	18	15
185	114	1	464	32	507
192	110	2	4625	44	3
213	34	136	471	53	15
259	69	952	492	100	712
2735	11	1010	499	105	1238
286	8	1104	4975	73	519
293	8	2003	506	100	712
300	7	3128	513	22	961
3005	7	3462	5115	54	519
Process Blue	7	3800	520	85	1239
313	20	3707	5185	58	58
3135	28	3644	527	22	724
320	41	3550	5255	8	736
327	7	3325	534	81	2036
3272	24	3675	5463	5	2764
3275	67	3363	5535	57	2252
3278	7	3090	562	80	2990
Green	76	3300	569	79	3095
340	8	2851	5747	20	603
3405	72	3096			

Biopolymers	A group of materials that share many of the physical properties of synthetic plastics, yet are derived from plants or bacteria. These materials are made of sugars, amino acids, and nucleotides, and are often biodegradable.
BPA	Bisphenol-a. An additive frequently found in polycarbonate plastic. A known endocrine disruptor.
CAMALS	Cadmium, arsenic, mercury, antimony, lead, selenium. A group of tightly regulated heavy metals.
Cause marketing	Type of marketing in which a business and a nonprofit advocacy organization work together for mutual benefit, or for social and charitable causes.
Cradle to Cradle	A description of waste-free, cyclical systems wherein all materials can be classified as either biological nutrients, which decompose naturally, or technical nutrients, which can be reused indefinitely.
CFL	Compact fluorescent lamp.
CSA	Community supported agriculture programs, wherein customers pay a set price for a weekly box of in-season fruits and vegetables directly from a farmer.
CSR	Corporate social responsibility. The idea that corporations must consider their impact on society and the environment in addition to their financial impacts. CSR reports are annual publications wherein corporations state their goals and performance relating to environmental and social measures.
De-inking	A phase in the recycling process during which ink is separated from paper fibers.
Downcycling	A recycling process that results in materials of a lower purity or quality than virgin materials.
ECF	Elemental chlorine-free bleaching. Paper pulp bleached with chlorine dioxide or other chlorine derivatives instead of elemental chlorine.
Embodied energy	The quantity of energy required to manufacture and transport a product or material to the end user.
EVA	Ethylene vinyl acetate. Conventional hot-melt glue used in "perfect" binding of books.
FSC	Forest Stewardship Council. An international not-for-profit membership-based organization that certifies forest products.
GHG	Greenhouse gas. Carbon dioxide, methane, nitrous oxide, and other GHG gases in the atmosphere tend to trap heat from the sun. Excess GHG emissions from human activities create instability in our planet's natural environment and contribute to global warming.
GMO	Genetically modified organism.
HAPS	Hazardous air pollutants. For a complete list see: *www.epa.gov/ttn/atw/188polls.html.*
HDPE	High-density polyethylene. #2 plastic.

HOV	High-occupancy vehicle lane. A highway lane reserved for vehicles with two or more passengers. Also known as carpool lanes.
Human factors	The observation and consideration of how humans relate to their environment, in hopes of improving the design of that environment.
Industrial Ecology	A process of integrating industrial systems so that they mimic cyclical systems found in nature. In such integrated systems, waste flows from one organization become productive inputs for other organizations.
LDPE	Low-density polyethylene. #4 plastic.
LED	Light-emitting diode. An energy efficient, long-lasting source of light increasingly used as a replacement for incandescent and fluorescent lighting sources.
LEED	Leadership in Energy and Environmental Design. A rating system for high performance green buildings, administered by the US Green Building Council.
Make-ready	The paper that commercial printers use while they adjust the ink levels and roller pressure on press. This is considered manufacturing waste and often represents up to 10% of paper used in a print run.
PC	Polycarbonate. #7 plastic.
PCF	Processed chlorine-free bleaching. Paper produced without elemental chlorine or chlorine derivatives. PCF applies to recycled paper fiber.
PCR	Post-consumer recycled. Paper fiber, plastics, and metals, derived from collection programs, that have previously been used at least once.
PCW	Post-consumer waste. See PCR.
PET	Polyethylene terephthalate. #1 plastic.
PHA	Polyhydroxyalkanoate. A biodegradable polyester biopolymer produced by bacterial fermentation of sugar or lipids.
PLA	Polylactic acid. A biodegradable polyester biopolymer, frequently derived from corn.
PP	Polypropylene. #5 plastic.
PS	Polystyrene. #6 plastic.
PUR	Polyurethane. A polymer found used in foams, varnishes, and adhesives. PUR adhesive is a stronger replacement for EVA "hot melt" in bookbinding.
PVA	Polyvinyl acetate. Used in adhesives for wood, paper, and fabric. Commonly used in bookbinding. Also known as white glue.
PVC	Polyvinyl chloride. #3 plastic.
RECs	Renewable Energy Certificates. A financial mechanism representing one megawatt-hour of renewable electricity production that can be sold and traded. RECs allow consumers to buy renewable energy without having a direct electrical connection to wind turbines, photovoltaic panels, or other sources of energy production.
Slow Food	Founded in Italy in opposition to "fast food" culture and lifestyle. Slow Food is now a worldwide organization concerned with healthy, fair, and sustainable agriculture and food preparation.

Sustainability	An environmental state that can be maintained indefinitely. Sustainable processes do not degrade the natural environment.
TCF	Totally Chlorine-Free bleaching. Paper produced without elemental chlorine or chlorine derivatives. TCF applies to virgin paper fiber.
TEF	Totally Effluent Free. A paper manufacturing process that releases little or no waste water. Also known as "closed-loop" manufacturing.
UV	Ultraviolet light. Electromagnetic radiation outside the range of visible light. UV inks include polymers that harden when exposed to ultraviolet light.
Variable Data Printing	A database-driven digital printing system that allows for customization of text and imagery within a large print run.
VERs	Verified emissions reductions. A financial mechanism representing a reduction or sequestration of one tonne of carbon dioxide or equivalent greenhouse gases. VERs vary greatly in their authenticity and are not tightly regulated. Also known as carbon offsets.
VOCs	Volatile Organic Compounds.

COMPANY	PAPER	FIBER CONTENT
UNCOATED (GREATER THAN 30% RECYCLED CONTENT)		
CASCADES FINE PAPERS	Rockland*	100% Recycled (100% PCR)
	Rolland Enviro100 Print/Book/Ecofibre	100% Recycled (100% PCR)
CRANE & COMPANY	Crest R*	100% Cotton (30% Post-Consumer Cloth
DALUM PAPIR	CyclusOffset	100% Recycled (100% PCR)
ECOSOURCE PAPER	ECO 21	40% Hemp, 40% Flax, 20% Cotton
FIBERMARK	Eviva	100% Recycled (30% PCR)
	Reprise	100% Recycled (30% PCR)
	Touche Cover	60% Recycled (20% PCR)
FRENCH PAPER	Construction*	100% Recycled (30% PCR)
	Dur-o-tone *	100% Recycled (30% PCR)
	Muscletone*	100% Recycled (30% PCR)
	Speckletone	100% Recycled (30% PCR)
GRAYS HARBOR	Harbor 100	100% Recycled (100% PCR)
	Quinault Opaque	100% Recycled (100% PCR)
GREEN FIELD PAPER	Hemp Heritage	25% Hemp, 75% PCR
LIVING TREE PAPER	Vanguard Recycled Plus	10% Hemp/Flax, 90% PCR
MOHAWK PAPER	Beckett Cambric*	100% Recycled (100% PCR)
	Beckett Concept*	100% Recycled (100% PCR)
	Options*	100% Recycled (100% PCR)
	Strathmore Script*	100% Recycled (100% PCR)
	Via*	100% Recycled (100% PCR)
MONADNOCK PAPER	Astrolite PC 100	100% Recycled (100% PCR)
NEENAH PAPER	Classic Crest Recycled*	100% Recycled (100% PCR)
	Environment PC100*	100% Recycled (100% PCR)
	Environment PC100 (Mesa White & Tortilla)	50% Sugar cane, 50% Recycled (30% PCR
	Fox River Select*	25% Cotton, 30% Recycled (30% PCR)
	Gilbert Cottons*	25% Cotton, 30% Recycled (30% PCR)
	Neutech*	25% Cotton, 30% Recycled (30% PCR)
NEW LEAF PAPER	Encore	100% Recycled (100% PCR)
	Everest	100% Recycled (100% PCR)
	Frontier	100% Recycled (100% PCR)
	Imagination	100% Recycled (100% PCR)
	Opaque	100% Recycled (100% PCR)
SMART PAPERS	Genesis*	100% Recycled (100% PCR)
	Passport*	50% Recycled (30% PCR)
	Proterra*	100% Recycled (100% PCR)
	Synergy*	100% Recycled (100% PCR)
SOUTHWORTH	Credentials Collection: Fine Recycled Paper	25% Cotton, 75% Recycled (50% PCR)
UNISOURCE CANADA	Save-A-Tree	100% Recycled (100% PCR)

LEGEND	* Indicates that only select colors within the grade meet the specifications shown.	**PCR** Post-Consumer Recycled

CHLORINE	CERTIFICATIONS	WEIGHTS	CONTACT INFO
ECF	EcoLogo	text, cover	www.environmentalbychoice.com | 800.388.0882
PCF	FSC, EcoLogo	text, cover	
		text	www.crane.com | 800.268.2281
PCF		text, cover	www.dalumpapir.com | +45 66117575
TCF		text, cover	www.islandnet.com/~ecodette/ecosource.htm | 800.665.6944
ECF		cover	www. fibermark.com | 800.327.8374
ECF, PCF		cover	
		cover	
PCF		text, cover	www.mrfrench.com | 269.683.1100
PCF		text, cover	
PCF		cover	
PCF		text, cover	
PCF	FSC	text	www. ghplp.com | 877.548.3424
PCF	FSC	text	
PCF		writing, text, cover	www.greenfieldpaper.com | 888.402.9979
PCF		text, cover	www. livingtreepaper.com | 800.309.2974
PCF	FSC	writing, text, cover	www. mohawkpaper.com | 800.843.6455
PCF	FSC	writing, text, cover	
PCF	FSC	text, cover	
PCF	FSC	writing, text, cover	
PCF	FSC	writing, text, cover	
PCF	FSC	text, cover	www.mpm.com | 800.221.2159
PCF	FSC	text, cover	www.neenahpaper.com | 800.994.5993
PCF	FSC	text, cover	
PCF	FSC	text, cover	
		text, cover	
		text, cover	
		text, cover	
PCF	FSC	copy	www. newleafpaper.com | 888.989.5323
PCF	FSC	writing, text, cover	
PCF	FSC	text	
PCF	FSC	writing, text, cover	
PCF	FSC	text, cover	
ECF	FSC	writing, text, cover	www. smartpapers.com | 800.443.9773
ECF	FSC	writing, text, cover	
ECF	FSC	writing, text, cover	
ECF	FSC	writing, text, cover	
		text	www. southworth.com | 800.225.1839
PCF		writing, text, cover	www.unisource.ca | 877.367.2904

PCF/TCF Unbleached or bleached without additional chlorine or chlorine derivatives
ECF Bleached with chlorine dioxide or other chlorine compounds
FSC Forest Stewardship Council Certified recycled or sustainably harvested virgin paper

COMPANY	PAPER	FIBER CONTENT
COATED		
APPLETON COATED	U2:XG	30% Recycled (30% PCR)
	Utopia One	10% Recycled (10% PCR)
	Utopia One X: Green	20% Recycled (20% PCR)
DALUM PAPIR	CyclusPrint	100% Recycled (100% PCR)
	RePrint	50% Recycled (50% PCR)
LIVING TREE PAPER	Déja Vu	10% Hemp/Flax, 60% Recycled (40% PC
MOHAWK PAPER	50/10*	15% Recycled (15% PCR)
NEW LEAF PAPER	Primavera	80% Recycled (60% PCR)
	Reincarnation Matte	100% Recycled (50% PCR)
	Sakura	100% Recycled (50% PCR)
NEW PAGE	ArborWeb	30% Recycled (30% PCR)
	ArborWeb Plus	30% Recycled (30% PCR)
SAPPI	Lustro Offset Environmental	50% Recycled (30% PCR)
SMART PAPERS	Knightkote Matte	50% Recycled (30% PCR)
	Kromekote C1S Recycled	50% Recycled (30% PCR)
SPICERS	Endeavour	50% Recycled (25% PCR)
UNISOURCE CANADA	Save-A-Tree Coated	100% Recycled (100% PCR)
WEST LINN	Nature Plus 30	30% Recycled (30% PCR)
COPY/REPROGRAPHIC		
BOISE INC	Aspen 100	100% Recycled (100% PCR)
	Aspen Color Copy	100% Recycled (100% PCR)
BPM INC	Envirographic 100	100% Recycled (100% PCR)
CASCADES FINE PAPERS	Rolland Enviro100 Copy	100% Recycled (100% PCR)
MOHAWK PAPER	Color copy 100% recycled	100% Recycled (100% PCR)
UNISOURCE CANADA	Save-A-Tree Copy	100% Recycled (100% PCR)
WAUSAU	Exact Eco 100	100% Recycled (100% PCR)
SPECIALTY		
COSTA RICA NATURAL PAPER	Banana/Cigar/Coffee/Lemon/Mango Paper	20% Agro-industrial fibre, 80% PCR
CTI PAPER USA	Glama Natural Recycled	30% Recycled (30% PCR)
FIBERMARK	Adirondack/Granada Cover	50% Recycled (15% PCR)
	Genuine Pressboard/Pressguard	60% Recycled (30% PCR)
GLATFELTER	Natures	30% Recycled (30% PCR)
	Thor PCW	30% Recycled (30% PCR)
MANISTIQUE	Manistique 100/Internet 100/Mystique	100% Recycled (40% PCR)
RED RIVER PAPER COMPANY	GreenPix	100% Recycled (100% PCR)

LEGEND

* Indicates that only select colors within the grade meet the specifications shown.

PCR Post-Consumer Recycled

CHLORINE	CERTIFICATIONS	WEIGHTS	CONTACT INFO
ECF	FSC	text, cover	www. appletoncoated.com	888.488.6742
ECF	FSC	text, cover	
ECF	FSC	text, cover	
PCF		text, cover	www.dalumpapir.com	+45 66117575
PCF	FSC	text, cover	
ECF	FSC	text, cover	www. livingtreepaper.com	800.309.2974
		text, cover	www. mohawkpaper.com	800.843.6455
ECF	FSC	text, cover	www. newleafpaper.com	888.989.5323
PCF		text, cover	
PCF		text, cover	
ECF	SFI	text, cover	www. newpagecorp.com	877.855.7243
ECF	SFI	text, cover	
ECF	FSC, SFI	text, cover	www.sappi.com	800.882.4332
ECF		text, cover	www. smartpapers.com	800.443.9773
ECF	FSC	text	
ECF	FSC	text, cover	www. spicers.com	800.774.2377
PCF		text, cover	www.unisource.ca	877.367.2904
ECF	FSC	text, cover	www.wlinpco.com	503.557.6500
PCF	FSC	copy	www.boiseinc.com	208.384.7000
PCF	FSC	copy	
PCF	FSC	copy	www.bpmpaper.com	800.826.0494
PCF	FSC, EcoLogo	copy	www.environmentalbychoice.com	800.388.0882
	FSC	copy	www. mohawkpaper.com	800.843.6455
PCF		copy	www.unisource.ca	877.367.2904
PCF	FSC	copy	www.wausaupapers.com	715.693.4470
PCF	FSC	text, cover	www.ecopaper.com	805.644.4462
ECF	FSC	translucent	www.thepapermill.com	800.284.7273
		leather-like cover	www. fibermark.com	800.327.8374
		tag board	
	FSC	book	www. glatfelter.com	866.744.7380
		book	
PCF	FSC	text, specialty	www.manistiquepapers.com	906.341.2175
PCF		inkjet photo matte	www.redriverpaper.com	888.248.8774

PCF/TCF Unbleached or bleached without additional chlorine or chlorine derivatives
ECF Bleached with chlorine dioxide or other chlorine compounds
FSC Forest Stewardship Council Certified recycled or sustainably harvested virgin paper

AIGA'S CARBONCOOL PROGRAM
*http://sustainability.aiga.org/content.cfm//sus_resources/
sus_greening/carboncool*

ALAMEDA GREEN BUILDING
www.stopwaste.org
Multi Family Green Building Guidelines
www.stopwaste.org/home/index.asp?page=291

AVEDA
www.aveda.com
Responsible Packaging
*http://aveda.aveda.com/aboutaveda/
responsible_packaging.asp*

BANNER CREATIONS
www.bannercreations.com

MICHAEL S. BROWN'S
SUSTAINABILITY TOOLKIT
www.bw-environmental.com/too.htm

DALUM PAPER
www.dalumpapir.com/866/734

EARTH DAY NETWORK
www.earthday.net/footprint.php

ECOENVELOPES
www.ecoenvelopes.com

ECO-FLEXX
www.eco-flexx.com

ECOSPUN
*www.wellmaninc.com/PolysterFibers/Branded%20
Products/EcoSpun/FortrelEcoSpunHome.aspx*

ECOSYNTHETIX
www.ecosynthetix.com

ELEPHANT PHARMACY
www.elephantpharmacy.com

U.S. ENVIRONMENTAL PROTECTION
AGENCY
www.epa.gov

EVERY MAN JACK
www.everymanjack.com

ENVIROSHELL FROM WINTERBORNE, INC.
www.enviroshell.com

FOREST STEWARDSHIP COUNCIL
www.fscus.org

FREE RANGE STUDIOS
www.freerangestudios.com

GLOBAL FOOTPRINT NETWORK
www.footprintnetwork.net

GREENBOTTLE
www.greenbottle.com

GREEN TEAM'S AFTER THESE MESSAGES
www.afterthesemessages.com

HP'S GLOBAL CITIZENSHIP REPORT
www.hp.com/go/report

KOHL & MADDEN
www.sunchemical.com/kandm

LEMNIS LIGHTING
www.lemnislighting.com

MARKETS INITIATIVE
www.marketsinitiative.org

MCDONOUGH BRAUNGART DESIGN
CHEMISTRY
www.mbdc.com

MIREL BIOPLASTICS
www.mirelplastics.com

MOHAWK PAPER
www.mohawkpaper.com

MONADNOCK PAPER
www.mpm.com

NATURAL LOGIC
www.natlogic.com

GREEN GRAPHIC DESIGN

THE NATURAL STEP
www.naturalstep.org

NATUREWORKS
www.natureworksllc.com

NEENAH PAPER
www.neenahpaper.com

NEW LEAF PAPER
www.newleafpaper.com

OPENECO
www.openeco.org

PANGEA ORGANICS
www.pangeaorganics.com

PAPER FOAM
www.paperfoam.com

PAPYRUS AUSTRALIA
www.papyrusaustralia.com.au

PHOENIX TECHNOLOGIES
www.phoenixtechnologies.net

PVC ALTERNATIVES DATABASE
http://archive.greenpeace.org/toxics/pvcdatabase/bad.html

R.I.T. PRINTING INDUSTRY CENTER—
RESEARCH INDEX
http://print.rit.edu/research/?page=monographs

RIVERDOG FARM
www.riverdogfarm.com

ROCKY MOUNTAIN INSTITUTE
www.rmi.org

SEAFOOD WATCH WALLET CARD
www.mbayaq.org/cr/cr_seafoodwatch/download.asp

SHUTTLEPOST
www.shuttlepost.com

SONOMA GRAPHIC PRODUCTS
www.sgpweb.com

SPIRAL BIND COMPANY
www.spiralbinding.com

STONYFIELD FARM
www.stonyfield.com

STRAUS FAMILY CREAMERY
www.strausfamilycreamery.com

STUDIO EG
www.studioeg.com

SUN MICROSYSTEMS
www.sun.com

SUSTAINABLE GROUP
www.sustainablegroup.net

TERRACHOICE—THE SIX SINS OF
GREENWASHING
*www.terrachoice.com/Home/Six%20Sins%20of%20
Greenwashing*

TERRACYCLE
www.terracycle.net

U.S. GREEN BUILDING COUNCIL
www.usgbc.org

VANCOUVER BOOKBINDING
www.ringbinder.com

WISDOM ADHESIVES
www.wisdomadhesives.com

WORLDCHANGING
www.worldchanging.com

1 WWF International, Zoological Society of London, Global Footprint Network. "Living Planet Report 2006." 2006. <www.footprintnetwork.org/download. php?id=303>.

2 Earth Day Network. "Ecological Footprint Calculator." <www.earthday.net/footprint.php>.

3 Casey, Susan. "Plastic Ocean: Our oceans are turning into plastic…are we?" *BestLife Magazine*. 25 Oct. 2007. 30 June 2008. <www.bestlifeonline.com/cms/publish/ health-fitness/Our_oceans_are_turning_into_plas- tic_are_we_2.shtml>.

4 State of Oregon Department of Environmental Quality. "Redesign Box Geometry." June 2005. <www.deq.state.or.us/lq/pubs/docs/sw/ packaging/bpboxgeometry.pdf>.

5 OECD. "Good Practice Greenhouse Gas Abatement Policies: Energy Supply and Transport." 2001. <www.oecd.org/dataoecd/39/52/1924144.pdf>.

6 Danish Environmental Protection Agency. "Ecolabelling of Printed Matter—Part II." 25 August 2006. <www2.mst.dk/Udgiv/publications/2006/ 87-7052-173-5/html/summary_eng.htm>.

7 Rothenberg, Sandra, Mary Anne Evans, and Sachin Kadam. "A Comparative Study of the Environmental Aspects of Lithographic and Digital Printing Processes." ReviseMay 2008. <http://hdl.handle.net/1850/1321>.

8 R.I.T. Printing Industry Center: Research Index <http://print.rit.edu/research/?page=monographs>.

9 World Resources Institute. "Last Frontier Forests: Ecosystems and Economies on the Edge." March 1997. <www.wri.org/publication/content/8563>.

10 Worldwatch Institute. "Worldwatch Paper #149: Paper Cuts: Recovering the Paper Landscape." 1 Dec. 1999. <www.worldwatch.org/node/841>.

11 Environmental Protection Agency. "Pollution Prevention Tips for You." <www.epa.gov/p2/pubs/tips.htm>.

12 Greenpeace. "PVC Alternatives Database." <http:// archive.greenpeace.org/toxics/pvcdatabase/bad.html>.

13 American Chemistry Council and the Association of Postconsumer Plastics Recyclers. "2005 Na- tional Post-Consumer Plastics Bottle Recycling Report" 2005. <www.plasticsrecycling.org/ documents/2005NationalPost-ConsumerPlastics BottleRecyclingReportFINAL.pdf>.

14 State of Oregon Department of Environmental Quality and U.S. EPA Environmentally Preferable Purchasing Program. "Lifecycle Inventory of Packaging Options for Shipment of Retail Mail-order Soft Goods." April 2004. <www.deq.state.or.us/lq/pubs/docs/sw/packaging/Life- CycleInventory.pdf>

15 Westervelt, Amy. "Back in the Saddle: L. Hunter Lovins." *Sustainable Industries*. 29 Feb. 2008. 30 June 2008. <www.sustainableindustries.com/ sijprofile/16123372.html?viewAll=y>.

16 Partners in Design. "EcoStrategies for Printed Commu- nications: An Information and Strategy Guide." 1996. <www.pidseattle.com/ECO/rescfaqs.html>

17 Telschow, Roger and U.S. EPA Office of Small and Disadvantaged Business Utilization. "Reducing Heavy Metal Content in Offset Printing Inks." April 1994.

BIBLIOGRAPHY

Chouinard, Yvon. *Let My People Go Surfing*. New York: Penguin Group, 2005.

Diamond, Jared. *Collapse: How Societies Choose to Fail or Succeed*. New York: Penguin Group, 2005.

Fuller, Buckminster. *Operating Manual for Spaceship Earth*. Carbondale: Southern Illinois University Press, 1969.

Hawken, Paul. *The Ecology of Commerce*. New York: HarperCollins, 1994.

Hawken, Paul, Amory Lovins, and L. Hunter Lovins. *Natural Capitalism: Creating the Next Industrial Revolution*. New York: Little, Brown and Company, 1999.

McDonough, William. *Cradle to Cradle: Remaking the Way We Make Things*. New York: North Point Press, 2002.

Morris, Helen. "Mills stamp out CO2 Emissions." PrintWeek. 9 Nov. 2007. <http://www.printweek.com/ news/765911/zmills-stamp-CO2-emissions/>.

Rothenberg, Sandra. "Environmental Management in Lithographic Printing." September 2002. <http://print.rit.edu/research/?page=item&id=81>.

Dr. Seuss. *The Lorax*. New York: Random House, 1971.

Todd, Nancy Jack and John Todd. *From Eco-cities to Living Machines: Principles of Ecological Design*. Berkeley: North Atlantic Books, 1993.

Van der Ryn, Sim. *Ecological Design*. Washington, D.C.: Island Press, 2007.

CREDITS

Page 65: © Pharos Project. Created by Jason F. McLennan and designed by Matthew A. Stiffler.

Photos by Terri Loewenthal pages: 90, 93, 176, and 178

Pen and ink illustrations by Patricia Katsura pages: 6, 11, 33, 37, 39, 41, 73, 76, 89, 95, 132, 184

Map on page 30 and illustration on page 142 by Yoonju Chung

Books from Allworth Press

Allworth Press is an imprint of Allworth Communications, Inc. Selected titles are listed below